A SCIENTIST EXPLORES SPIRIT

A BIOGRAPHY OF

EMANUEL SWEDENBORG

WITH KEY CONCEPTS OF HIS THEOLOGY

GEORGE F. DOLE & ROBERT H. KIRVEN

Chrysalis Books
Imprint of the Swedenborg Foundation
West Chester, Pennsylvania

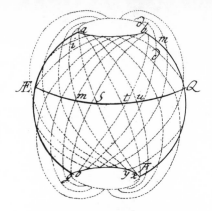

*A particle created by the rapid spiral motions
of a more elementary particle. Swedenborg's
drawing shows the large globular particle
as the sum of the motions (from* Principia, *1734).*

Copyright 1997, Swedenborg Foundation
Library of Congress Cataloging-in-Publication Data
Dole, George F. A scientist explores spirit: a biography
of Emanuel Swedenborg with key concepts of his theology/
George F. Dole and Robert H. Kirven

p. cm.

Originally published: New York: West Chester, Pa.:
Swedenborg Foundation, 1992
Includes bibliographical references and index.
ISBN 0-87785-241-3
1. Swedenborg, Emanuel, 1688–1772.
2. Mystics—Sweden—Biography.
I. Kirven, Robert H.   II. Title.
[BX8748.D65   1997]
289.4'092—dc21
[B]   97-614
CIP

BOOK DESIGN: CAROL S. LAWSON
TYPESETTING: SUSANNA V. R. LAWSON

This biography
is based on Robert H. Kirven and Robin Larsen's
"Emanuel Swedenborg: A Pictorial Biography"
and George F. Dole's "Key Concepts in Swedenborg's Theology"
and "A Rationale for Swedenborg's Writing Sequence, 1745–1771,"
which appeared in Robin Larsen, et al., eds.
Emanuel Swedenborg, 1688–1772: A Continuing Vision.
New York: Swedenborg Foundation, 1988. Most of the illustrations
in the present volume are from the 1988 biography
and are available in the
Swedenborg Image Archive at the Foundation.

Contents

Introduction
A Scientist Explores Spirit, vii

Swedenborg the Scientist Explores Spirit
Ferment at Uppsala, 3
Old Swedberg, 7
Independent Studies Abroad, 13
In Service to Charles XII, 19
Swedenborg: Assessor and Statesman, 23
Swedenborg: Author and Publisher, 27
Scientific Works, 31
More Studies Abroad, 33
The Turning Point, 37
Spiritual Experiences, 41
Theological Writings, 45
Apocalypse and Theology, 49
Controversies, 53
Real Religion, 57
Final Journey, 61
The Dilemma Resolved, 63

Key Concepts in Swedenborg's Theology, 65
God, 66
Our Humanity, 67
Love, 68
Human Process, 68
Revelation, 69
Correspondence, 70
Universality, 71
Immortality, 71
Maximus Homo, 72
Incarnation, 72
A Radical Claim, 73
A Vision, 74

Notes, 75

Bibliography, 79

Illustration Sources, 83

Emanuel Swedenborg: Life Chronology, 85

Index, 95

Descriptio.

Machina Volatilis et Portatilea.

A SCIENTIST
EXPLORES SPIRIT

On March 25, 1744, Emanuel Swedenborg recorded a dream from the previous night in his diary:

> [I] stood behind a machine, that was set in motion
> by a wheel; the spokes entangled me more and
> more and carried me up so that it was impossible
> to escape; wakened.[1]

He was fifty-six years old at the time, and in his waking hours he was in fact deeply enmeshed in detailed research and writing on the subject of human anatomy in an effort to identify the seat of the soul. Undeniably a brilliant and successful man, he was engaged in an immense and complex task, but the dream suggests that he was beginning to feel trapped by his own intellectual prowess. Events would soon reveal that he was on the verge of a profound and far-reaching change that would indeed "carry him up" into adventures in levels of knowledge and understanding he could not foresee even by contemplating his remarkable dreams. Since his student days at Uppsala University, he had been entranced by the mechanistic view of the universe offered by Descartes and Newton—so entranced that his writings revealed little trace of the intensely personal religion of his childhood. Now he was beginning to recognize that loss and to wrestle with its implications. The question he faced can be

Two centuries before the Wright brothers' flight, in 1714 Swedenborg designed a machine to fly in the air. These are his notes and sketch for his aircraft (left).

simply stated: to maintain the religious faith he treasured, did he have to give up the scientific intellect he also treasured?

In this respect, he was a particularly intense embodiment of his culture. He had grown up at a time when religion's dominance in the world of thought was beginning to be challenged by science. The struggle was borne in on him by prominent players in the changes that marked the era. The dream may well reflect his years as assistant to Christopher Polhem, then Sweden's greatest engineer; his close association with John Flamsteed, one of England's greatest astronomers; and his visits with many of the best known researchers and mathematicians in England and on the continent. But the two strongest influences during the first third of his life were arguably his father, Jesper Swedberg, and his school, Uppsala University.

During Emanuel's childhood, his father, Jesper Swedenberg was dean of the Cathedral and professor of theology at the University of Uppsala. This view of Uppsala shows the cathedral in the left background, the university buildings, and the castle in the right background.

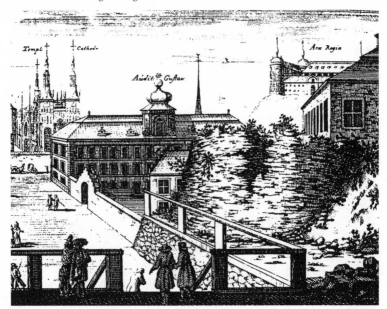

A Scientist
Explores Spirit

Ferment at Uppsala

To appreciate the cultural influences and political climate of Sweden when Swedenborg was a youth, we need to understand that at the time of his birth in 1688, the Swedish empire included all the major ports ringing the Baltic Sea—parts of modern Finland, Latvia, Poland, Denmark, and Germany. During Swedberg's young adulthood, Charles XII would first extend these boundaries by hundreds of miles, and then lose all he had gained and more, plunging the country into crisis and bringing about a decisive rejection of absolute monarchy.

The wave of intellectual excitement that became known as the Enlightenment was spreading to Sweden from Germany and England. For a quarter-century before Emanuel's birth, the academic and religious communities of Uppsala had been involved in a heated argument: one side wanted to allow "Cartesianism"—the freedom of inquiry championed by the philosopher Descartes, who had visited Sweden shortly before his death there in 1650, while the other strove to maintain the old ways of teaching only what was approved by the church. In 1689, before Emanuel was two, Charles XI decreed that while the church tradition should continue to be the supreme authority for the theology faculty, all other departments of the university should be permitted complete freedom of inquiry. Excitement ran high.

While Emanuel was at Uppsala, Hebrew was intro-

The Charles Academy and the Royal Academy Hospital at Uppsala.

duced to the curriculum, and students were suddenly exposed to the vast world of rabbinical scholarship. It was taught by Johan Kemper, a converted Jew and Kabbalist, who shared with many Jews and Christians a sense that the millennium was at hand; in fact he had turned to Jesus as the Messiah after having been disappointed in a contemporary Jewish claimant to the title. Elsewhere in the middle of the seventeenth century, Oliver Cromwell and the British parliament had encouraged the immigration of Jews into England for the explicit purpose of meeting one of the preconditions for the coming of the Messiah—helping the Jews to scatter to all the ends of the earth!

In that intellectual climate, scientific inquiry was high adventure. A younger contemporary, Linnaeus, would do definitive botanical work in the first comprehensive classification of plants. In the same atmosphere, one of the most eminent professors, Olof Rudbeck, could (1) teach mechanics in order to modernize the mining industry and (2) write a massive work tracing the Swedes back through the Goths to the inhabitants of Atlantis, proving their superiority to all other nations and their manifest right to rule the continent.

Rudbeck, professor of medicine and botany at Uppsala and an early champion of Cartesianism, was a friend of the Swedberg family. In a great fire which raged through Uppsala in 1702, he is credited with directing students who saved most of the books in the university library and many of Jesper Swedberg's books as well. It was presumably his son and namesake who instilled a deep interest in botany and anatomy in two of his most famous students—Swedberg and Linnaeus—and also guided them to a fascination with what today would be called comparative religions, including the religious symbols of antiquity and Lappish shamanism. From Rudbeck also may have come the passion for grand, overarching systems which both men followed so productively.

The royal decree of April 17, 1689, was obeyed in practice at Uppsala, but continued to be the subject of vigorous theoretical debate. In these arguments between Cartesianism and "Aristotelianism" (a popular code-word for Lutheran conservatism), one of the most articulate Cartesians was the university librarian, Erik Benzelius. Jesper Swedberg was an equally passionate spokesman for the Aristotelian view. Emanuel's older sister, Anna, married Erik Benzelius in 1703, and when Jesper left Uppsala that summer to take up his duties as Bishop of Skara, Emanuel lived with Erik and Anna for his remaining years at the university. At school and at home, he formed such a close relationship with Benzelius that he loved and revered him "as a father."[2] For much of his life, he continued to wrestle with the tension between the scientific approach to life espoused by his second father and the obedience to faith championed by his birth father.

The Enlightenment had not filtered down far enough to challenge what we would now see as widespread popular superstition. Angelic and demonic presences were facts of life, confirmed by tales of miraculous happenings. In the household of Emanuel's childhood, and in his father's sermons, these were taken as wholly consonant with a Christian faith, indeed as essential to it.

Imagine an intense intellect plunged into the midst of this ferment: nothing is more important than the Christian faith and the Bible that reveals it; nothing is more exciting than the empirical investigation of the physical world. In such a context, sudden shifts of focus are natural. The unexpected is to be expected.

The mature Swedenborg would amply fulfill this expectation, but we have no record of big surprises during

5

Emanuel's student days. He entered the university at eleven—not especially remarkable at the time, particularly for gifted students with important family connections. His father and his prospective brother-in-law were ideally placed: he also had ancestral ties to the same great mining corporation that supported a number of boys from his part of the country. He was surely as much a part of Sweden's industrial, economic, and intellectual establishment as any of his classmates. Also, he had advantages like pre-admission tutoring from an older cousin, Johan Moraeus. Trained as a pharmacist and soon to study medicine in Paris, Moraeus provided exemplary guidance for young Emanuel's interest in science.

Raised in a mine-owning family, Swedenborg was familiar with the work of miners, shown above in the Great Copper Mountain Mine at Falun, near the Swedberg ancestral home. As a government official, Swedenborg worked to make the mines both more productive for Sweden and safer places for miners to work.

Old Swedberg

Jesper Swedberg was thirty-five and a chaplain to the court of King Charles XI when Emanuel was born; he died, a doctor of theology and the bishop of Skara, when Emanuel was forty-seven. Jesper and his older brother Peter were the first generation of the family to bear a family name instead of a traditional Swedish patronym: Jesper's father, a wealthy mine owner, was Daniel Isaacsson, his father was Isaac Nilsson, and his was Nils Ottesson, and so on. When Daniel Isaacsson chose a family name for his sons, he called them "Swedberg," perhaps because the family farm and homestead near the Great Copper Mountain mine at Falun was called Sveden (*Svedens Gard*, or "burned farm," cleared by fire from the surrounding forest).

Emanuel was born in Stockholm on January 29, 1688, the third of nine children of Jesper and Sara (Behm) Swedberg. He was the second son, but his older brother, Albert, died when Emanuel was eight, leaving him the eldest surviving male of his generation. Two of his sisters—Anna, two years older, and Hedwig, two years younger—remained especially close to him, each providing a home for him at different periods of his life. A younger brother, Daniel, died when Emanuel was only three; and the next brother, Eliezer, died when Emanuel was twenty-eight. A sister Katharina and brother Jesper both lived for seventy-seven years but died before Swedenborg. Emanuel was survived by only his

In Swedenborg's lifetime, Stockholm, seen here from the west, was Sweden's capital and largest city. A lakeport and seaport with miles of shoreline, its many bridges connected the outlying parts to the central island of the Old Town (Gamla Stan)—site of the

youngest sister, Margaretha. The birth dates of all the Swedberg children were recorded according to the Julian calendar, which was used in Sweden until 1740. If the Gregorian calendar, in use throughout the world today, were retrojected to that time, the dates would be 11 days later: Emanuel's birthday would be February 9.

Emanuel's baptism took place in the small Jakobs Kyrka in Stockholm on February 2, 1688, the same day that Princess Ulrika Eleonora, a future queen of Sweden, also received the church's baptism.

Jesper served as a court chaplain in Stockholm during the first four years of Emanuel's life. The chancel of the Royal Chapel offered a magnificent pulpit for an impassioned preacher, and Jesper Swedberg used it so well that Charles XI once warned him he had many enemies—to which Jesper replied, "A servant of the Lord is not good for much, if he has no enemies."[3]

royal court and government offices, including the Board of Mines where Swedenborg served as assessor.

The future bishop apparently had no fear of making enemies. He took strong, unpopular stands on a host of issues, ranging from opposition to elaborate hairstyles for women, to writing and publishing a hymnal that his fellow clergy refused to adopt. He taught his children that spirits in the room observed every word and action. He particularly stressed the conviction (generally called "Pietism") that living a Christian life is more important than the more orthodox Lutheran virtue of doctrinal faith—"brain faith," according to Jesper. He is said to have read at the dinner table every night from Johann Arndt's *True Christianity*, a large work often called "the bible of Pietism."

When Emanuel was four years old, Charles XI appointed Jesper to the faculty of the University of Uppsala as professor of theology. That had become a sensitive position, since disputes continued to rage between the theological faculty and all the others. Unable to challenge Charles's decree, Aristotelians and Cartesians continued trying to convince each other regarding the appropriate principle for supreme academic authority.

Two years later, Jesper was given the additional post of rector of Uppsala Cathedral. The frequent academic and theological discussions in his home led Emanuel in later years to recall this as a time when he "was constantly engaged in thoughts on God, salvation, and the spiritual sufferings of men."[4]

He also remembered that, from age twelve (as a university student), he started to "delight in conversing with clergymen about faith,"[5] and experimented with hypoventilation or minimal breathing, which he would later observe as characteristic of his states of intense concentration.[6]

In 1696, Emanuel's eighth year, both his mother and older brother died from a fever. About a year later, Jesper married again, this time to Sara Bergia, daughter of another wealthy miner. It was less than six years later that he moved to Brunsbo, leaving Emanuel in Uppsala with Anna and Erik. Although Emanuel lived with his stepmother for little more than five years before she moved to Brunsbo, he appears to have become her favorite among her six stepchildren.

During the thirty-three years that Jesper lived in Brunsbo, Emanuel visited his father often. On one of these visits, he installed a speaking tube to the kitchen, said to have been used for ordering coffee. Other times, he is said to have helped his father plant three or four of the great old trees which still stand around the house. Although the two may have disagreed over Emanuel's career choice,[7] there are many signs like this of the son's affection for his father. The affection may have been reciprocated, but we know more about Jesper's eloquence in the pulpit than about his demonstrations of personal affection.

Jesper did return to Uppsala from Brunsbo to hear Emanuel's dissertation defense in 1709. In those days, the defense was regarded as so much more important than the dissertation itself that some students hired faculty members to do the writing. Emanuel, however, wrote his own—*Selected Sentences from L. Annaeus Seneca and Publius Syrus the Mime, with notes*—and defended it to everyone's satisfaction. If we need any evidence that he did not receive a twentieth-century education, this will surely do: mastery of classical secular literature was taken to be a good foundation for a career in the natural sciences.

This portrait of Swedenborg in his nineteenth year was painted about 1707. He had blue eyes.

Swedenborg's First Trip to the Continent

Independent Studies Abroad

Sweden in 1709 offered no opportunities for advanced engineering studies. Charles XII had succeeded Charles XI in 1697, and was engaged in his Russian campaign—the disastrous attempt that diminished the empire and severely depleted the treasury. The country was under attack from Denmark, and France was trying to blockade England, severely curtailing contacts with foreign countries. A series of crop failures brought the country close to famine, and bubonic plague was beginning to spread across Sweden. Neither the comfortable manse at Brunsbo nor Sweden itself offered opportunity or enticement to the young graduate. So the next summer, at age 22, he sailed for England.

It proved to be a risky decision, seriously threatening Emanuel's life four times during the journey: once in a fog at sea, when his ship came so near a sand bank that "all [aboard] considered themselves lost";[8] again when it was boarded by French privateers who thought the ship was British, while the passengers feared the attackers were Norwegian; yet again when, mistaken for a French privateer, the ship was fired on broadside by an English warship; and once more—most seriously—in London.

This last danger arose when the ship lay quarantined in London harbor because of the plague in Sweden, and the impetuous youth accepted an invitation from Swedish friends in London to jump ship and land in spite of the quarantine. Arrested and threatened with hanging, he escaped death only by excellent recommendations, the intervention of friends, and great good luck.

The dome of St. Paul's Cathedral dominated the skyline of Swedenborg's London.

London in 1710 was a world center of learning and culture, vastly larger and more cosmopolitan than any city young Swedberg had seen, offering countless opportunities for new experience and learning. This was the era of Queen Anne, the Augustan age of art and literature. The city had been rebuilt after the great fire of 1666, and St. Paul's Cathedral had just been completed. In science, London was the hub of the Newtonian revolution, a magnet for adventurous minds.

Free at last to continue his education and faced with a marvelous menu of possibilities, Emanuel proved omnivorous. By taking lodgings with craftsmen, he simultaneously lived more cheaply than in conventional rooms and learned the crafts of his hosts—watchmaking, cabinet making, brass-instrument making, and engraving. At the same time, he purchased books and equipment unavailable in Sweden to teach himself chemistry by performing Boyle's experiments.

He also served as a purchasing agent for his university, helping to bring its library and equipment up to date. He read Newton daily, and he sought out the company of other young scientists and mathematicians in London's coffee houses.

From London, he moved on to Greenwich and made the acquaintance of the master of the observatory there, John Flamsteed. This happened to be the period in which Flamsteed was absorbed in the thousands of precise telescopic observations that would produce the first detailed tables of the positions of the moon. Emanuel's interest and ability led to his becoming Flamsteed's assistant, making nighttime observations and recording data. Here he began working on a method of determining longitude at sea by means of the moon and also conceived a dream he would cherish for years—of establishing an astronomical observatory in Sweden.

The Octagon Room at the Royal Greenwich Observatory
(below) where Swedenborg became assistant
to the master of the observatory.

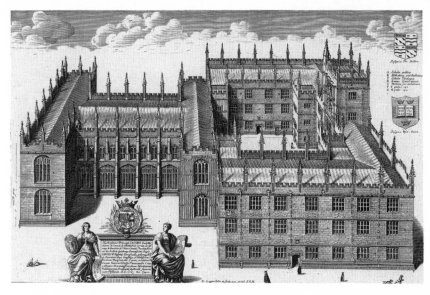

The Bodleian Library, Oxford, in the eighteenth century.

More than a year after his arrival in England, a second allowance of money from home enabled him to move to Oxford, where he met with the other great astronomer of the time, Sir Edmund Halley. Halley discouraged him in his longitude-finding method based on Flamsteed's tables, perhaps reflecting a professional jealousy that appears to have existed between Halley and Flamsteed.

While at Oxford, he visited the Bodleian Library and met its librarian, Dr. John Hudson, who had been corresponding with Erik Benzelius. He shifted his focus from science for while and devoted himself to the English poets, even writing some Latin poetry himself. His interests lay more with science than with literature, however, and soon led him on to the continent.

In Leiden, Emanuel studied science and scientific equipment at the university, taking special note of the magnificent observatory there. He visited the pioneering microscopist Anton van Leeuwenhoek, whose observations he often would cite later in his physiological writings. He found lodging with a lens grinder, who taught him the techniques of that trade in exchange for assistance in the laboratory. With that skill, plus the brass-instrument making he had learned in London, he made for himself (or had made under his personal direction) a microscope modelled after an instrument he had seen in van Leeuwenhoek's laboratory—except that van Leeuwenhoek's was 20-power, and Swedberg's 42-power. The microscope was a much-prized treasure: earlier, in London, he had written to Benzelius that he had looked at one for sale, which "I would have bought . . . if the price had not been so much higher than I could venture to pay."[9]

From Leiden, he travelled to Utrecht, where leaders were gathered for the 1712 Peace Congress, which eventually settled a number of small wars (including the one that Emanuel had sailed through in 1710) and brought peace to western Europe. Here we find the first clear evidence of political interests that would inform a significant part of his later life. He met with ambassadors from Sweden and other countries, such as England's Bishop John Robinson. Moving next to Paris, he met with the leading French scientists of the time and visited Versailles, admiring the beauty of the marble statues in the magnificent palace gardens.

When he headed homeward after four years, he paused for several months in Rostock (then a Swedish possession on the southern coast of the Baltic Sea) to gather his notes and drawings into something he could show for his travels. Although most of his studies on the trip had been in chemistry, astronomy, mathematics, and poetry, he did have a notebook filled with mechanical inventions. There were fourteen items

Swedenborg's microscope and case.

in all, several of them devices to ease the work of Swedish laborers. Many were inventions for use in mining, reflecting the influence of his teacher Rudbeck and the mining interests of the Swedbergs, Behms, and Bergias. There were mechanical hoists to make work safer for the miners, and other engineering devices to improve the efficiency of Sweden's major industry.[10] Other inventions were more theoretical—impressive examples of a contemporary fashion among inventors, such as a machine to fly in the air.[11]

The airplane was especially noteworthy. Its fixed wing with a true airfoil, the cockpit for a pilot, and the landing gear were all firsts in aircraft design. The young inventor had calculated accurately the wing surface necessary to support the craft, and recognized the need for invention of an adequate source of motive power. He also recognized the gap between a design based on theory and a machine that would work, warning that "when the first trials are to be made, you may have to pay for the experience and must not mind an arm or a leg."[12]

In November 1714, Charles XII ended his Russian campaign by escaping from a Turkish prison and completing a heroic march of 1250 miles in fifteen days to come to the defense of the Swedish outpost Stralsund on the south coast of the Baltic, east of Rostock. Emanuel wrote an ode in celebration of the event, *Festivus Applausus in Caroli XII . . . Adventum,* with some remarkably ingenious interpretations of his monarch's failures in appropriately oratorical Latin. Then he set sail for home.

In Service to Charles XII

Back in Sweden, young Swedberg spent his first six months living with his father and stepmother at one of the family estates: Starbo, in central Sweden west of Uppsala. He had completed university studies and a European sojourn, requisites for a well-educated Swede. Now, what could he do with his knowledge and abilities? Of his many dreams, only one came to fruition. This was Sweden's first scientific journal, which he named *Daedalus Hyperboreus* ("Northern Daedalus") after Greek mythology's father of inventors—the first human to fly. He prepared the first issue in Starbo, and after a Christmas vacation with Erik Benzelius joined Christopher Polhem and his family at Stjarnsund in January 1716.

Polhem soon became another important figure in his life. He was Emanuel's senior by twenty-seven years, and was already known as Sweden's most famous inventor, attracting visitors and students from Sweden and Europe. Emanuel had hoped to join Polhem as an apprentice on his graduation from Uppsala, but the opportunity to visit England had come first. Twenty-eight years old now, with five years' study abroad under famous teachers and a notebook full of inventions, he could join Polhem more as an assistant than as an apprentice.

The great inventor was pleased with the new journal (nearly every issue of which featured a Polhem invention), and delighted with his new assistant. He involved Emanuel in his work and soon offered him the hand of his oldest daughter Maria. Emanuel, however, preferred Maria's younger sister Emerentia and employed what he called "some intrigues" to avoid marrying Maria while keeping himself in everyone's good graces. But Emerentia refused him, desiring to marry another. Though deeply disappointed (Emerentia was brilliant and capable as well as beautiful: after her father's death, she assumed management of the forge at Stjarnsund), Emanuel continued working for Polhem.

Meanwhile, King Charles XII had commissioned Polhem to build a drydock projected as one of the greatest in Europe. The dock was to be at Karlscrona on the southern tip of the Swedish peninsula. On his way there, Polhem visited the king at Lund, where Charles had set up a temporary headquarters in preparation for an attack on Norway, and introduced his assistant, Swedberg. Emanuel had held a low opinion of Charles, but took an immediate personal liking to him when they actually met. The king had abundant charm and a lively and inquiring mind, and the two had many long conversations about science and mathematics. Although Charles took little interest in *A New Method of Finding the Longitudes of Places, on Land, or at Sea by Lunar Observations,* which Emanuel also published at this time (1718), he admired Swedberg's *Daedalus Hyperboreus,* and a textbook in geometry written by Polhem, which Swedberg had published.

At Polhem's request, the king rewarded Swedberg with an appointment to a government position. Emanuel chose a post as special assessor (unpaid member) on Sweden's Board of Mines. Though this irregular appointment would not be translated into a salaried job for over a decade, the post was a natural one. The Swedberg family owned shares in the Falun Mine, one of Sweden's largest sources of copper. The Stora Kopparberg (Great Copper Mountain [Corporation]), operator of the Falun Mine, is in fact one of the oldest corporations in the world. Long established even in the early 1700s, the corporation provided the fortunes of many of the families that formed the economic, social, and political backbone of the country. Emanuel's mother, Sara Behm Swedberg, was the daughter of Albrecht Behm, another wealthy mine owner—with an interest in Stora Kopparberg and other mines—and a member of the Board of Mines. His stepmother, Sara Bergia, owned shares in the Stora Kopparberg as well.

Charles also engaged Polhem and Swedberg to build a canal linking Stockholm with the North Sea, thus avoiding the strait that was vulnerable to control by Denmark. The project was complicated by steep grades over rugged mountains. Eventually completed only in this century, the Trollhattan Canal now passes within sight of an abandoned portion known as "Polhem's Sluice," which Emanuel was helping with in the summer of 1718. That summer found him occupied as well with work on the Karlskrona drydock and Sweden's first saltworks. During this period, he also devised a method by which, under his supervision, Charles's navy moved some ships fifteen miles overland to defeat the Norwegian navy defending the Norwegian stronghold of Fredrikshald.

Charles XII was laying siege to Fredrikshald in November 1718. Swedberg again had used what he called "intrigues," this time to avoid serving in the campaign[13]; and he appears—for that or another reason—to have fallen somewhat out of favor with the monarch. On November 30, however, Charles's favor suddenly became irrelevant, for a bullet to the royal head abruptly ended his reign. Historians have never been sure whether the shot came from a Norwegian soldier or a Swedish assassin; but Sweden was thrown into mourning—and a search for a new ruler.

The Swedenborg family coat-of-arms, in orangey-reds, blue, and brown, dates from his ennoblement in 1719.

Swedenborg: Assessor and Statesman

On March 17, 1719, the Swedish crown was bestowed on Ulrika Eleonora, younger sister of Charles XII—the princess baptized on the same day as Emanuel Swedberg. She gained the throne despite the claim of another candidate, her nephew Charles Frederick of Holstein-Gottorp, partly because she happened to be in the country at the time and partly because her husband Fredrik was in the trenches when Charles died and could immediately proclaim her queen. Fredrik also arrested Charles's prime minister (Baron Görtz, widely

Riddarhuset, the Swedish House of Nobles, was faithfully attended by Swedenborg for fifty-three years.

hated and later beheaded for his brutal extortion of taxes to finance Charles' campaigns). Perhaps most significantly, Ulrika was willing to renounce the absolute rule enjoyed by Charles, and agreed to govern jointly with a Council of the Realm. The following year, she would relinquish the throne to her husband (with the same constitutional limitations).

On May 23, 1719, in a move which strengthened her position in the parliamentary House of Clergy and increased the number of her supporters in the House of Nobles, she ennobled the families of Sweden's bishops. Emanuel's name was changed from Swedberg to Swedenborg, and his life changed in other ways as well.

As the eldest male in his generation of the family, he was entitled to a seat in the *Riddarhus* (House of Nobles), one of four houses of the *Riksdag* (Parliament) which governed the country jointly with the queen. The new nobleman took his seat immediately and remained an active and diligent member. Except when his travels for study and publication took him out of the country, Emanuel attended Riddarhus sessions regularly for the rest of his life. Although he spoke seldom, if ever, in the House (apparently he considered himself a poor speaker because of a speech impediment), he wrote a number of papers that were published for distribution to the nobles. Many of these papers have been preserved. For the 1722–1723 Riksdag, for instance, he published five pamphlets. They dealt with currency reform, balance of trade, priorities in mining noble and base metals, developing iron production, and establishing rolling mills. His last major contribution, an extensive 1771 paper on Swedish currency, only months before his death, reprinted his 1722 currency-reform paper and added an equal amount of new text. Swedenborg's fifty-three years of service in the Riddarhus (1719 to 1772) coincided almost exactly with Sweden's Age of Freedom, the interim between the absolute monarchy of Charles XII and the reestablishment of absolute royalty by Gustav III in a coup on August 19, 1772, six months after Swedenborg's death.

Lars Benzelstierna (born Lars Benzelius in 1680, and ennobled at the same time as Swedenborg) was the brother of Emanuel's brother-in-law, Erik Benzelius, and was manager of smelters on the estate of Swedenborg's mother, Sara Behm—the ironworks at Axmar, Starbo, and Skinnskatteberg. Benzelstierna married Swedenborg's younger sister, Hedwig. Lars and Emanuel worked in the same office for many years, and for some of those years, Hedwig and Lars provided a home for Emanuel at Starbo, their home on Lake Barken in Dalarna.

While at Starbo in March 1719, Swedenborg learned that his stepmother, Sara Bergia, had died of pneumonia at Brunsbo on March 3. Jesper was married for the third and last time some eighteen months later to Christina Arrhusia, daughter of the dean of Falun.

Sara Bergia's will left seven heirs and five other claimants. Lars and Emanuel each received one-seventh of Sara Bergia's estate and one-fifth of half of Sara Behm's—the other half going to their aunt, Brita Behm. Emanuel and Lars bought out the other shareholders and held joint custody of Starbo, which Lars continued to manage.

The third portion of the Behm inheritance, Axmar, included the ironworks, vast forests to supply wood for the charcoal used in smelting, and a long stretch of coastline with its own harbor. The Axmar Ironworks was operated alternately by agents of Brita Behm and agents of the minor shareholders, and disputes between these agents led to a series of lawsuits by Brita against the others. Swedenborg led the negotiations with his aunt Brita, and suspected Benzelstierna of instigating the suits. When the whole affair was settled, Swedenborg was left with an adequate income for life.

After much bureaucratic maneuvering, during which Benzelstierna and two other men received salaried posts ahead of Swedenborg, Swedenborg eventually gained a permanent, salaried seat on the Board of Mines in 1724. He was to serve full-time as an active member for twenty-three years, until he retired from the board in 1747 to devote his energies to theological writing. By that time, he had become so well accepted by the board that he was nominated for promotion from assessor to councillor on the Board of Mines (his eulogy in 1772 was delivered by a councillor of mines).

The job he now held was by no means a sinecure. In its meetings, the board formulated policies for Sweden's most important industry and adjudicated what were often complex and bitter legal disputes. Both of these tasks required a thorough knowledge of the facts involved. Further, the board was charged with the responsibility of inspecting the mines themselves; and in order to do this effectively, members had to know how things worked on the most practical level. Swedenborg took a particular interest in this latter area. He was to devote a great deal of time and energy to modernizing the industry, and once he was thoroughly familiar with the problems and with the procedures of the board, he went in search of solutions.

Emanuel Svedenborg

Author and Publisher

After five years at home, then, Swedenborg travelled again on the continent, now pursuing studies which led to the publication of a *Preface to the Principles of Chemistry*. He passed through Copenhagen, open to Swedes after several years because a peace treaty was about to be signed, sailing from there to Hamburg. Continuing through the now familiar cities of Leiden and The Hague, he visited sites where he could admire the architecture of Europe or observe the commercial and industrial methods of the different countries, such as the smelting plants in Aachen (also known as Aix-la-Chapelle). He particularly sought out mining and smelting centers, like those in Liege, where he could enlarge his expertise in what had become his principal career interest—increasing his value to the Board of Mines.

He not only studied European methods which might be useful for the kinds of mining and smelting then practiced in Sweden, but also concentrated on industries that might be started up at home—rolling mills near Cologne, and a stamping mill at Altenberg. Since all of Sweden's metals had to be exported for finishing, European mills garnered large revenues that Swedenborg wished to keep in Sweden.

Swedenborg's plans included extensive publication, so on this trip he also took a special interest in printing. In

Leipzig, he found one of the continent's premier presses, Friedrich Hekel, to which he would return on his next trip with a manuscript in hand ready for printing.

Returning to Stockholm, Swedenborg took up his life as a nobleman, bureaucrat, and author. He worked daily at the Board of Mines, except when travelling to inspect mines or smelters—often in company with Lars Benzelstierna. Whenever the Riksdag met, he sat in the Riddarhus, writing detailed papers for the nobles and other houses of the Riksdag. Three preserved papers are *The Balance of Trade* and *The Inflation and Deflation of Swedish Money,* and for the Board of Mines, *Noble and Base Metals.* Deeply involved in his government work and his scientific manuscripts, he declined nomination to a full professorship at Uppsala—a position which became available when his old astronomy teacher, Nils Celsius, retired.

In 1724, he helped to establish a Museum of Technology in Stockholm and a Museum of Mining in Falun. Many of the early exhibits were models of inventions by his former mentor, Christopher Polhem, and some of those models—still on display—were built by Swedenborg. In 1725, he became a mentor himself, taking under his wing Erik Benzelius, Jr. (son of his brother-in-law, Erik Benzelius) whom he instructed in physics and mathematics.

During these years he courted a young woman of seventeen, Kristina Maria Steuch, daughter of the bishop of Karlstadt and descended from another bishop and three archbishops. "Stina Maja," as she was called, is known to have had at least three suitors at the time—Swedenborg; a Magister Arnell, preferred by her father; and Chamberlain Cedercreutz, whom she preferred. When she married Cedercreutz, Swedenborg's family pointed out another eligible and pretty prospect for marriage, but he does not appear to have courted her, or anyone else.

He did have a close friend in Elisabet Stierncrona. She was the wife of Count Gustav Fredrik Gyllenborg, who had been a friend of Swedenborg's for almost thirty years. A colleague of Emanuel in the Riddarhus, he had advanced from being King Fredrik's chamberlain to having become one of the most powerful politicians in Sweden as well as a fellow assessor on the Board of Mines. His benevolence brought him into financial troubles later, and he died in 1759 owing a substantial sum of money to Swedenborg. Elisabet had married Gyllenborg in 1729, when she was fifteen and Swedenborg was forty-one. The couple remained his close friends throughout the count's life, often visiting him in the home he later purchased on the street called Hornsgatan. Swedenborg's friendship with Elisabet continued until her death in 1769.

In 1728, his sister Hedwig died, and he moved into an apartment at 7 Stora Nygatan. He hired a servant and settled into the life of a bachelor. His nephew and pupil, Erik Benzelius, Jr., lived with him for part of this time and began to follow his uncle's footsteps by studying metallurgy. Erik was eventually to join his uncles Emanuel and Lars on the Board of Mines.

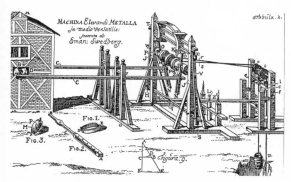

This hoisting machine, invented by Swedenborg, raised the ore out of mines more efficiently and safely than the traditional method in which miners had to carry the ore up ladders.

Swedenborg's drawings from **Principia** show the evolution of planets.
From top left to lower right, the solar crust surrounding
the sun before breakup; the breakup of the crust
with some parts moving inward and others outward;
the gathering of planetary material
after the crust collapses into a zone;
and the final emergence of planetary bodies.

Scientific Works

After eleven years in Stockholm, during which he established himself in the Riksdag and the Board of Mines, Swedenborg completed the manuscript for his biggest work so far and travelled again in May 1733 to Germany to see it though the press. This, his third foreign trip, was the only one on which he sailed directly from Stockholm to Europe instead of travelling overland to a Swedish port closer to the continent. He got from Stockholm to Berlin in a week, arriving in Berlin on June 2.

Then he spent June, July, and August in Dresden and Prague, putting finishing touches on his manuscript. The three-volume set was entitled *Philosophical and Mineralogical Works*, and the individual volumes were: *I. First Principles of Natural Things, II. On Iron and Steel,* and *III. On Copper and Brass.*

The first volume was devoted to an overarching cosmology, including both a nebular hypothesis and a remarkable atomic theory, and setting these significantly in a kind of theological framework. The two mineralogical volumes established Swedenborg as one of the world's leading experts in mining and smelting, the area of his professional focus for twenty-three years on Sweden's Board of Mines. The third volume of *Philosophical and Mineralogical Works* also included a picture of a fossil, excavated by Swedenborg from the side of Mount Kinnekulle almost twenty years earlier. Discovery of the fossil had led to his hypothesis published in his 1718 work, *On the Height of Waters and Strong Tides in the Primeval World,* claiming that the highest mountain in Sweden once had been under water. That work establishes Swedenborg as one of the first to publish a theory consistent with modern geology.

On September 3, 1733, he arrived in Leipzig and turned his manuscript over to the printer Friedrich Hekel. Seeing the new work through early proofs to final publication took several months, extending into 1734. During this visit, he sat for a portrait by an engraver, which was used as the frontispiece of the first volume. It is used also as the frontispiece of the present biography.

That portrait, executed in Leipzig in the fall of 1733 for publication close to his birthday in 1734, shows Swedenborg at the end of his forty-fifth year. It is the picture of a man confident of himself and of his place as one the leading European philosophers of his time.

In July 1735, about a year after Emanuel's third return to Sweden (he was now well-known in Europe because of the favorable reviews in the German press of his *Philosophical and Mineralogical Works),* his father died. Jesper Swedberg had been bishop of Skara for thirty-three years, a doctor of theology for thirty years, and was widely admired and loved, despite having made many enemies with his outspoken preaching and ministry. The funeral at Varnhem in Westrogothia near Skara was held in January 1736, and his body was laid to rest at Varnhem Cloister.

Paris Observatory

More Studies Abroad

We are left to speculate on Emanuel's feelings about his father's death, but we can see a significant shift of focus in his work. After two years at home, during which he published a small but adventurous work linking theoretical physics to human anatomy and sensation, *On Tremulation*, Swedenborg left for Europe again. This trip was for more than four years, so he contributed half his salary at the Board of Mines to be distributed among three fellow-members who would assume his duties in his absence. Once again, he passed through Linköping to spend a few days with Erik and Anna Benzelius (Benzelius had been appointed bishop there), and then travelled through Copenhagen to Amsterdam.

He spent summer 1738 in Amsterdam, where he enjoyed the atmosphere of political freedom but disliked what he described as the prevalent attitude of greed among the people of this commercial and cosmopolitan country. He began what he planned to be a large work identifying the seat of the soul. This was a popular effort among philosophers of his day, but Swedenborg's approach was distinctive. He embarked on an intensive study of human anatomy, concentrating on the recent discoveries from the dissection laboratories of Leeuwenhoek, Malpighi, Ruysch, Bidloo, Vieussens, and Boerhaave. Working with intense concentration, aided by the hypoventilation that he had used to help himself concentrate in early childhood, he felt assured that his thoughts were on the right track when he experienced what he called "a sign": "... a certain cheering light and joyful flash ... a certain mysterious radiation—I know not whence it springs—that darts through some sacred temple of the brain."[14] The first records of these flashes of approval appear as diary entries during this visit to Amsterdam. ✓

Not all of Swedenborg's time was spent in writing and meditation. In the fall of 1739, he sent a table inlaid with marble home from Amsterdam, where he had watched the craftsman make it. His fascination with the process is recorded in a paper he wrote about it, published by the Swedish Royal Academy of Sciences in 1763.[15] The table is now in the Kommerscollegium (Board of Commerce) on Riddarholmen, which housed the Board of Mines for a short time after Swedenborg's death.

In the autumn, he moved on to Paris. He took rooms on the Rue de l'Observatoire where he could renew acquaintances with some of the French astronomers he had worked with on his last visit, twenty-three years before—rooms just a short walk from Paris' new School of Surgery and Dissection, where he sat in on a number of lectures. He had some experience with dissection instruments, and the possibility of new discoveries in this comparatively new field held a strong attraction for his inquiring mind, but that very attraction raised a caution flag for him. He decided to rely on the dissections of others for his new physiological work because he anticipated that he might be inclined to give undue importance to anything that he happened to discover: he could be more objective using the published work from other laboratories.[16]

He left Paris and travelled to Italy the following spring,

arriving in Torino in time to see the parades re-enacting the Passion scenes. Moving on through Milan to Venice, he visited the Plaza of St. Mark's at the time of the annual celebration of the marriage between the doge and the sea. His travel diaries show that everywhere he went, he visited all the best-known architectural wonders and centers of learning, such as the University of Padua. They suggest that he had finished at least the first draft of his *Economy of the Animal Kingdom* ("Dynamics of the Soul's Domain") surveying the body as the domain of the soul, and was looking ahead to a future work on the brain.

In Rome, he visited the Colosseum and all the other famous historical sites, as well as the great art galleries and the Vatican library (where his *Philosophical and Mineralogical Works* were kept on the Proscribed Index). Then, journeying back through Paris to Amsterdam, he finally finished *Economy of the Animal Kingdom* and sent it to the printer.

After the press run was completed, he took some copies with him and headed for home. He spent several days in Copenhagen, studying in the libraries and accepting invitations from people of scientific or social distinction.

At this period of his life, Swedenborg moved in the highest circles of Swedish society. He was regularly present at the Riksdag when it was in session, and frequently in attendance at the royal court. Among his friends were men such as Executive Councillor Count von Hopken and House of Nobles President Count Tessin.[17]

On December 10, 1740, Swedenborg was accepted into the Swedish Academy of Sciences, joining Tessin, von Hopken, and Linnaeus, who had been its founding members the year before. Carolus Linnaeus, often called the father of modern botany, was married in the guest house of Swedenborg's ancestral home, Sveden, to the daughter of Johan

Moraeus (Swedenborg's cousin who had tutored him as a youth). There are other indications of mutual respect and personal acquaintance between Swedenborg and Linnaeus, but no details concerning their friendship.

On July 21, 1743, Swedenborg went on his fifth trip abroad, this time to publish the first two volumes of a massive work he had planned on the *Animal Kingdom* ("The Soul's Domain"), a more detailed study of the body than *Economy of the Animal Kingdom*. He had come to the painful conclusion that this latter work had been too superficial to serve his purpose, and that a much more detailed investigation of the body would be necessary to identify the seat of the soul on purely empirical grounds. *Animal Kingdom*, for which he produced first drafts of separate volumes on the brain, the nervous system, the reproductive system, and other parts and systems of the human body, marked the high point of his physiological studies. His achievements in the field of anatomy were now substantial, including the accurate identification of areas of the brain controlling specific motor functions and the discovery of the functions of the ductless glands.

For the publication of all but his smallest works, Swedenborg had to travel to the continent, because Sweden had no printing facilities capable of large-scale printing jobs of the quality offered by the presses Swedenborg is known to have used in Amsterdam, Leipzig, The Hague, and London. He may also have been sensitive to the fact that church authorities regularly scrutinized manuscripts for theological errors and that his deeper speculations on the nature of the human soul might well be regarded as heretical. The press he chose for *Animal Kingdom* was in The Hague.

The Turning Point

The spring of 1744 was marked by severe emotional conflict in Swedenborg's life. To all appearances, he was highly successful. He had a secure, high-level government post, an international reputation as a scientist, and entrée to the highest social circles; but he also had a growing sense of impending crisis. He continued to work as usual, but inwardly he moved between unaccustomed exhilaration and depressing self-criticism; and his nights were filled with such strange dreams that he began recording them in a travel diary. That diary, known in English as his *Journal of Dreams*, records his dreams over some twenty-one months in 1743–1744. The accounts are terse and candid, usually with a brief sentence stating the meaning he attached to the dream when he woke. These dreams (including the one described at the beginning of this biography) suggest a growing awareness of involvement in a great process beyond his control. His comments on them show him struggling during that winter and into spring 1744 with a sense of religious inadequacy. Among other pressures, his father's religious heritage clamored for recognition, and he took it seriously.

While the typesetting and press work were in progress, he took the manuscript of his next volume to work on while he travelled from The Hague to nearby Dutch cities. He took rooms in Amsterdam and attended Easter Sunday services there on April 6, 1744, the next day moving on to Delft. He

397.

398.

Swedenborg's record of his "turning point" appears in two diaries—a travel diary, and a larger one he kept at home. Entry 397, above, is from the latter, now known as his Spiritual Diary, and refers to the London theophany.

had experienced intense inner turmoil over the Easter weekend, but during his journey on Monday, he enjoyed a wonderful feeling of bliss.[18]

That night, he suddenly was seized with such trembling that he fell from his bed onto the floor. There, feeling wide awake, he experienced a Christ-vision. He found himself cradled in Jesus' arms and felt that he had been divinely commissioned to a special work. Struggling after the experience with doubts of his worthiness for such a visitation, countered by a fear of sinning if he doubted his Lord, he eventually felt gifted with a comforting certainty, and fell at last into a peaceful sleep.[19] Before morning, he dreamed that his father came to him and without speaking a word, tied the ribbons of his cuffs. Waking, Swedenborg wrote down all the events of the night, concluding with this dream and noting that lace cuffs were a symbol of laity: his father tying the ribbons of them symbolized for him that his father approved of him (at last) in a life outside the clergy. The dream signalled another change in him, as well: he had come to regard his father as an equal, rather than an authority.[20]

This vision of the Lord left him with a strong sense of commission, but apparently without a clear sense of direction. He wrote *Worship and Love of God*, a striking, poetic blend of mythology and science, but published only part of it. Perhaps he was making use of an accepted literary device to begin to communicate his new-found and growing meaning, as yet not feeling ready to "lay it on the line." There is a posthumous, third-hand report that he said of this work that "it was certainly founded on truth, but somewhat of egotism had introduced itself, as he had made a playful use of the Latin language, on account of his having been ridiculed for the simplicity of his Latin style in later years."[21]

Another theophany, in London in spring 1745, greatly

clarified his understanding of his commission. Here, as he later described it to friends, he had the first of his open and conscious experiences of the spiritual world and conversations with its inhabitants, "so that I became thoroughly convinced of their reality." Here also, the Lord appeared "in imperial purple and majestic light, seated near his bed, while he gave [Swedenborg] his commission," and told him, in the course of about a quarter of an hour, that his specific task was to "explain to men the spiritual meaning of Scripture."[22]

In his subsequent manuscripts, these two foci—spiritual experience and biblical understanding—are clearly and separately represented. A very substantial "Bible Index" shows what we would expect of a good Lutheran, commissioned to explain Scripture and convinced that "the Word" was the sole source of revealed truth. The "Spiritual Diary," a faithful record of his other-world experiences, testifies to the impact that these encounters were having on his thought. These manuscripts were to serve as basic resources for his later writing—the man of faith and the empiricist were beginning to work hand in hand.

After the London vision, he abandoned all his studies of mathematics and physiology, and within a year resigned at half-salary from the Board of Mines (at the time he was offered a promotion from assessor to councillor).

This ended the second phase of a life that falls into rough thirds. From his birth until the death of Charles XII, he spent thirty-two years as a student and an engineer. Then came twenty-four years as administrator, statesman, and scientist. After a year of transition, the remaining twenty-seven years of his life were devoted primarily to an adventurous spiritual search—revelatory spiritual experiences, Bible study, and theological writing. He remained socially accessible and active in politics, however, throughout his life.

Spiritual Experiences

Returning home from London in 1745, Swedenborg moved from his apartment to a house he had purchased on Hornsgatan. There, when not travelling abroad, he lived and wrote for the rest of his life. Perhaps his new sense of commission made him feel more permanently settled or perhaps he felt a need for greater privacy during his spiritual experiences, which were occurring every day and sometimes lasted for hours. In any case, he gave every sign of settling in. He planted an herb-garden. He built a summer house connected to a library room where he could work in surroundings more pleasant than the dark, crowded rooms necessitated by Swedish winters. Within the summer house he had a chamber organ built which he used for meditative playing.

The Bible Index begun then led to a commentary on the five "Books of Moses" (Genesis–Deuteronomy), Isaiah, and fifty of the fifty-two chapters of Jeremiah, a work later called *The Word Explained.* Evidently he intended to write a commentary on the entire Bible, but after completing several codices of manuscript (nine volumes in English translation) he left the work unfinished.

Swedenborg enjoyed working in this little summer house

There is some evidence that the extensive *Spiritual Diary,* also begun in 1745, originally was intended for publication; but the format of the manuscript is not up to his usual standard for submission to a printer, and his notes to himself indicate that he had in mind considerable editorial work. He eventually indexed it, and drew on it quite freely for other works.

While Swedenborg's spiritual experiences and his understanding of the Bible are in fact closely related and mutually supportive, these two foci of attention remained distinguishable. We can see Swedenborg immediately after his call following two related but quite distinct tracks, and devoting a good deal of time and energy to each.

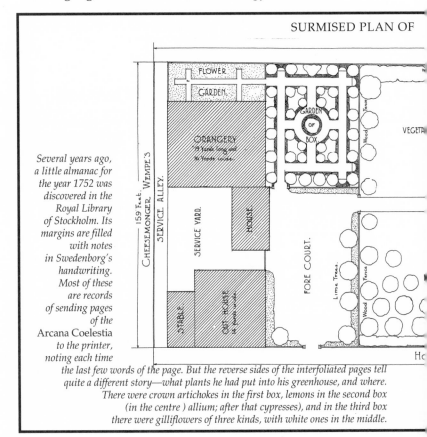

SURMISED PLAN OF

Several years ago, a little almanac for the year 1752 was discovered in the Royal Library of Stockholm. Its margins are filled with notes in Swedenborg's handwriting. Most of these are records of sending pages of the Arcana Coelestia to the printer, noting each time the last few words of the page. But the reverse sides of the interfoliated pages tell quite a different story—what plants he had put into his greenhouse, and where. There were crown artichokes in the first box, lemons in the second box (in the centre) allium; after that cypresses), and in the third box there were gilliflowers of three kinds, with white ones in the middle.

The new kind of information he was gaining from his spiritual experiences began leading him to a new conception of reality. Eventually, his new understanding would treat knowledge from spiritual and natural experience as fully compatible, encompassing not only these two tracks, but also his father's faith and Uppsala's science, in one coherent whole.

At this point, however, scripture exegesis came to the fore, as might be expected from his understanding of his commission. The years 1749–1756 saw the publication in London of the eight folio volumes of *Arcana Coelestia* ("Heavenly Mysteries"), a commentary on the books of Genesis and Exo-

SWEDENBORG'S PROPERTY IN STOCKHOLM

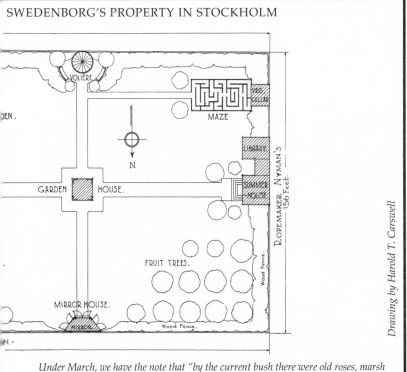

Drawing by Harold T. Carswell

Under March, we have the note that "by the current bush there were old roses, marsh mallows, and gilliflowers of a curious kind; parsley and beets, spinach and carrots." In the rose bed were African roses and velvet roses, and beside them lilies, rose-mallows, and sunflowers. And always the notes about printing the Arcana.

dus. The spiritual meaning "unfolded" in this massive work deals with three primary themes: the interaction of the divine and the human in the life of Jesus; the checkered history of the spiritual states of humanity; and to some extent issues of spiritual growth in individuals. Perhaps the clearest indication of his initial intent appears in the beginning of his printer's advertisement: "This work is intended to be such an exposition of the whole Bible, as was never attempted in any language."

He did not ignore his spiritual experiences, though. Between chapters, he inserted a serial description of the spiritual world based on what he had seen and heard. His spiritual experiences were too intimately connected to his understanding of Scripture to be ignored. As the work progressed, he began to use this "interchapter" space for more systematic explanation of theological themes. This first work uses his three primary modes of presentation—scriptural interpretation, narration, and doctrinal exposition.

Throughout the work—as throughout all his theological works—he took pains to assure the reader that what he wrote was not the figment of imagination or devisings of his own brain. The spiritual experiences were real and coherent, and the doctrines were given him "not from any angel, but from the Lord."[23] He was no mere secretary, since he saw his extensive scientific development as preparation for this commission; but the essential message he was delivering was God's gift and not his own achievement.

Theological Writings

At this point, Swedenborg was faced with a decision. In dealing with Genesis, he had covered, at least in outline, the whole course of the Lord's glorification (his term for the process by which God became human and this human became the Risen Lord or Divine-Human); in dealing with Exodus he had dealt with much of the history of religion. It is hard to imagine how he could have kept on the same course much longer; the deciding factor may have been that *Arcana Coelestia* was not selling well, even at substantially subsidized prices and with publication of an English translation of the second volume. The message was not getting out.

Whatever the reason, Swedenborg completed his treatment of Exodus and stopped the work without any appropriate conclusion. He then turned to other forms of presentation. Two years after the publication of the last volume of the *Arcana*, no fewer than five separate works were written and published, drawing heavily on the *Arcana*. *The White Horse of the Apocalypse* is a treatise on the nature of the Word, with copious *Arcana* references. *The New Jerusalem and Its Heavenly Doctrine* is a kind of theological glossary, with extensive *Arcana* extracts appended to each brief chapter. *Earths in the Universe* is a description of the inhabitants of other planets, lightly edited from *Arcana*'s interchapter material, while *Heaven and Hell* is an expanded treatment of subjects introduced in the same way.

Prospectus Horti Regii qui Holmiæ est, ambulacris et arborum plantarumque.
ex remotis orbis partibus advectarum, varietate amœnissimi, versus Septentrionem.

Between sessions of the senate and the Board of Mines, Swedenborg no doubt often visited the Royal Gardens in Stockholm (above). Whether at home, working on manuscripts, or traveling in Holland, land of tulips, or in England, country of roses—wherever he might be, Swedenborg's horticultural interests, his garden planning and seed hunting were ever in mind. It has been conjectured that he may have received the seeds of the American plants for his garden because of his interest in the Swedish Academy of Sciences to which he belonged (see the garden arrangement on pp. 42–43).

Three works also rest heavily on Swedenborg's spiritual experiences. Material that was secondary in the *Arcana* now takes center stage for a while. The former two works *(White Horse* and *New Jerusalem and its Heavenly Doctrine)* show a clear theological orientation. Material that was scattered through the exegesis of Genesis and Exodus is now gathered together in topical arrangement (the same concern for topical rather than scriptural ordering is of course represented in Swedenborg's two indices to the *Arcana).* The three modes of presentation have emerged in separate works.

These five works are far smaller, and their substance is far more accessible than *Arcana Coelestia. Heaven and Hell,* written to "dispel disbelief" in our spiritual natures and our immortality, has proved to be the most popular of Swedenborg's works, and both *Earths in the Universe* and *The Last Judgment* appealed in subject and title to contemporary interests. It is difficult not to believe that the commercial failure of *Arcana Coelestia* was a factor in this change of approach. Swedenborg did, after all, want his works to be read.

The Last Judgment also had a unique motive for publication—the opportunity to report its actual occurrence! The work dealt, indeed, with the Last Judgment foretold in the Book of Revelation, but described it as an historical event which Swedenborg had witnessed in his spiritual experiences during the year 1757. He saw it as the end of the Christian church as a living institution, paving the way for the Lord's Second Coming prophesied in the Gospels, and the establishment of a new church in the world. In this view, the scriptural descriptions should not be taken as literal prophecies of the destruction of the physical world, but as symbolic descriptions of the end of a thought-world. Some two centuries before it became intellectually fashionable, Swedenborg announced the beginning of the post-Christian era!

To publish these five works, Swedenborg left for England on his seventh trip abroad in the summer of 1758. On the way home in July 1759, he landed at Gothenburg, on Sweden's west coast, some 300 miles from Stockholm. An event there attracted the attention of all Sweden and much of Europe.

On the night of July 19 he was entertained at dinner in the home of William Castel, a prominent Gothenburg merchant. During the meal he became very agitated, leaving the table several times. He told the dinner guests that a great fire was raging in Stockholm at that very moment, and each time he returned to the table he described the progress of the blaze, eventually relating with great relief how the fire had been stopped close to his house without damaging it. Within a few days, a ship from Stockholm brought news of the fire, exactly coinciding with Swedenborg's description. Word of his clairvoyance began circulating throughout the country.

Queen Louisa Ulrika heard the story, and talked to him about it in a private audience. She asked him if he could contact her brother, the recently deceased King August William of Prussia, and Swedenborg agreed to try. A few days later, he came to the court, requesting another private audience. After he spoke a few words to her, the queen appeared shocked, and exclaimed, "This no mortal could have told me!"[24] The stories of the Stockholm fire, the queen's secret, and another concerning a lost receipt reached the continent, and were described in 1763 by Immanuel Kant in a letter to a patroness, Charlotte von Knobloch. In response to her inquiry, Kant had done some research into Swedenborg's character, and gave an essentially favorable report, which was widely circulated.

Apocalypse and Theology

As soon as the five smaller works were off the press, Swedenborg turned back to Scripture. Abandoning any thought of writing a commentary on the entire Bible, he turned from Genesis and Exodus to the last book, Revelation, also known as the Apocalypse, and began writing *The Apocalypse Explained*. He got about halfway through the nineteenth chapter out of twenty-two and then laid it aside. It is a major work, comprising six substantial volumes in English translation; and various opinions have been advanced as to his reasons for dropping it.[25]

The main reason can perhaps be seen in the nature of the work itself. Through much of it, Swedenborg stuck quite close to his exegetical program, though more discursively than in the *Arcana*. Early in his treatment of Revelation 15, however, he began to attend to another task. Whereas in the *Arcana* he had inserted material between chapters, he now appended material to each numbered paragraph. This "secondary" material, which he called "continuations," gradually grew in scope, and the exegetical material became more and more cursory. The scriptural focus was being replaced, this time not by an experiential focus, but by one on topical or systematic theology.

The result is awkward. Suppose you are involved in

reading two books concurrently. It is one thing to read a chapter of one and then a chapter of the other, along the model of the *Arcana.* It is quite another thing to read a paragraph of one and then a paragraph of the other. Consecutive reading toward the close of *The Apocalypse Explained* becomes increasingly difficult for the same reason. Perhaps we need look no further for Swedenborg's reason for laying the work aside.

By this time, Swedenborg was known not only for his philosophical and mining publications and his telepathic powers, but also for his theological writings. Count Gustav Bonde, a senator and past president of the Board of Mines, now chancellor of the University of Uppsala, had discovered the preceding January that Swedenborg was the author of *Arcana Coelestia,* which had been published anonymously. Count Tessin, a friend of Count Bonde and Swedenborg, held dinner meetings of a circle of Stockholm artists and literati at his beautiful seacoast home, Svindersvik. In 1760, he invited Swedenborg to join the group, giving him an opportunity for discovering first-hand how he was being understood.

In the fall of 1760, devastating critiques of *Arcana Coelestia* and *The White Horse* were published in Germany by a leading biblical scholar, Professor Johann Ernesti, who mistook Swedenborg's spiritual interpretations of the Bible for the allegorical method that was incompatible with orthodox literalism.[26] In the same year, another prominent theological scholar and writer, Friederich Christoph Oetinger, who had written favorably about Swedenborg's theological works, found himself under attack, and formulated an extended defense of Swedenborg—*Swedenborg and Others Compared*—that attracted wide attention.

It is estimated that Swedenborg stopped working on *The*

Apocalypse Explained in 1759. In 1763, he published no less than six books—the *Four Doctrines* (*The Lord, Sacred Scripture, Life,* and *Faith*), *A Continuation on the Last Judgment,* and *Divine Love and Wisdom;* and in 1764 he published *Divine Providence.* Much of this material is clearly foreshadowed in the "continuations" in *The Apocalypse Explained.*

Now, however, there is a new dimension to the shift of focus. Swedenborg's preface to the first of these 1763 works, *The Doctrine of the Lord,* lists five "little works" already published, and nine more that he is to publish "by command of the Lord." Swedenborg was reasonably obedient to this command, publishing seven of the nine works listed, and in fact covering all the topics involved. It is worth particular note that in four of them (today found in one volume, *The Four Doctrines*) he is as concerned to present their biblical foundations as to explain them systematically, making a case for his teachings in terms that held particular authority for his fellow Lutherans. In sharp contrast to this, there is very little biblical material in *Divine Love and Wisdom* or *Divine Providence.* The biblical emphasis and the polemical tone of parts of *The Four Doctrines* may have been in response to criticisms like those of Ernesti; but in any case, he seems deliberately to be keeping his agendas separate.

At this point, we can gain a clearer view of the process. If we put the nature of *The Apocalypse Explained* together with the command to write recorded in *The Doctrine of the Lord,* then the "continuations" can be seen as a kind of premonition of the command. They are evidence that Swedenborg was beginning to pick up a message concerning the specific direction his work should take, a direction different from the biblical one that was foremost in his consciousness.

Swedenborg apparently felt free to follow the listing of books he had been commanded to write in principle rather than in complete detail. It is also worth special note that in listing the works published "some years ago," Swedenborg did not mention the *Arcana*—a rather substantial omission, since at that time it represented about two-thirds of his published theology. There could scarcely be a clearer indication that he regarded the 1763–64 works as being in the same "special category" as the five works published in 1758, quite distinct from his "explicit" task of scripture exegesis.

When *Divine Providence* was published in 1764, then, Swedenborg evidently felt both free and commissioned to return to the apocalypse. The freedom is witnessed by his very single-minded and efficient exegesis. The commission may have been the quite explicit one he recorded in *Marriage Love.* At the close of an account of a spiritual experience (undated), he says, "Then I heard a voice from heaven, `Go into your room, close the door, and get down to the work you started on the *Apocalypse.* Carry it to completion within two years.'"[27] A new work under a slightly revised title, *The Apocalypse Revealed,* was in fact published in 1766, two years after the publication of *Divine Providence.*

In following Swedenborg into the next world, it is easy to assume that he had retired from this one. But he remained an amiable and sociable man of independent means and a welcome guest at dinner parties and country homes such as Svidersvik.

Immanuel Kant (1724–1804)

Controversies

The criticism that most damaged Swedenborg's reputation was published in 1766 in Germany by Immanuel Kant under the title *Dreams of a Spirit-Seer*. In the years since Kant's 1763 letter to Fraülein von Knobloch, he had purchased and read *Arcana Coelestia* and now condemned it as "eight quarto volumes full of nonsense." Kant appears to have been deliberately ambiguous in this and many of his other critical comments. On the one hand, he called the work "nonsense," but on the other hand said that none of its data was *sense* datum! Claiming that only a madman would write things which could not be proved, Kant savagely criticizes the work with witty if occasionally crude ridicule, but includes a curious comment::

> It's my bad luck that the testimony I have stumbled
> on . . . so uncommonly resembles my own brain
> child. . . . However sarcastic the comparisons may
> turn out, I intend no joke. I want to make it as clear
> as I can that either there is more intelligence and

truth in Swedenborg's works than a first glance will reveal, or else it is only an accident that he coincides with my system.[28]

Kant apparently had this "resemblance" in mind when he explained the violence of his attack in a letter to a friend, saying that he thought it better "to ridicule than to be ridiculed." Shortly thereafter he began work on his own *Critique of Pure Reason* (finally published in 1781), setting forth ground-rules for philosophy on an entirely different basis from Swedenborg's. Self-serving as it was, his attack on Swedenborg proved so effective that for generations it was impossible for any German scholar to speak favorably of Swedenborg and be taken seriously.[29]

There is no indication that Swedenborg was aware of this criticism as he turned to another subject which had been on his mind for years—the spiritual dimensions of marriage. This had been given brief but distinctive treatment in the first of his published theological works, *Arcana Coelestia*, and there is a chapter on "Marriages in Heaven" in *Heaven and Hell*. In *The Doctrine of Life* he had mentioned his intent to write on the subject; and in the book he was now to publish, he spoke of a command from heaven to "write" what he had learned about marriage. On April 9, 1766, he received a letter from a friend and supporter, Dr. Gabriel Beyer of the Gothenburg Consistory, expressing a wish for such a book.[30]

Swedenborg apparently had made one or more starts on the project, and now brought it to completion. In several respects, the resulting work broke with his established patterns. It was the first of his theological works to bear his name on its title page, even though the secret had been out for at least eight years, during which seven works had been published. When defending it against confiscation as a heretical book, he himself described it as "not a theological work, but mostly a book of morals";[31] and no other work keeps such an insistent focus, in its expository sections, on human behavior and circumstances. No other work has such a high proportion of narrative to exposition. Swedenborg chose the title "Delights of Wisdom" in preference to the "Angelic Wisdom" or "Doctrine of . . ." which appear in other titles. Further, the device of opening with an extended description of spiritual events, especially one of high whimsy, is quite without precedent in his other works.

Marriage Love was published in 1768. Swedenborg was then eighty years old. His age itself must have militated against undertaking another major exegetical task, and circumstances began to press him in another direction. Since the time around 1760 when his authorship of his theological works had become known, criticism of their theology began to be addressed more directly to him, and there were the beginnings of formal criticism from some quarters in the Lutheran hierarchy. Now his few followers were meeting the opposition from the established church that would culminate in the dispute which began in Gothenburg that fall.

Arriving in Gothenburg in 1769, after his tenth European trip, he found that two influential leaders in that city—Bishop Erik Lamberg and Dean Olof Ekebom—were heading a campaign to have his books declared heretical. They succeeded in confiscating one box of *Marriage Love,* and raised charges of heresy against two of his friends and supporters seriously enough to threaten their jobs. The two friends were the Dr. Beyer already mentioned and Dr. Johan Rosen, professor of eloquence and poetry at the University of Lund. Each found himself under severe pressure to renounce Swedenborgian teachings; but because of their own eloquent defense and support from various well-connected supporters of Swedenborg, neither was actually forced from his position.

William Blake, reader of Swedenborg and champion of the apocalyptic changes—scientific, political, social—taking place in the late eighteenth century, drew upon Swedenborg's New Jerusalem visions, as in "Los Entering the Grave" frontispiece for his epic poem Jerusalem.

Real Religion

It may come as no surprise, then, that we find Swedenborg suddenly occupied with the study of standard Christian doctrine. His working manuscripts now deal with such topics as "Justification and Good Works," "A Conversation with Calvin," and "Remission of Sins." In 1769 he directly addressed the relationship of the new theology to the old in *A Brief Exposition*. In sharp contrast, *Soul–Body Interaction*, published in the same year, is exclusively "philosophical," dealing with none of the issues raised at the heresy trial. This may represent another instance of his deliberately keeping his agendas—or perhaps more precisely, his audiences—separate.

It is, in a way, a short step from *A Brief Exposition* to his last published work, *True Christian Religion*. Effectively, it responds to the hostile critique of his theology by orthodox Lutherans. Swedenborg had hitherto been concerned more to present the new theology than to defend it. He had followed the course of Scripture, he had shared his spiritual experiences, and he had dealt with specific and timely topics. He now seems convinced that he needed to address the growing opposition from orthodox Lutheranism even more directly than he had in *Arcana Coelestia* and the *Four Doctrines*.

To do so, he needed to rely on authorities whom the Lutheran church regarded as valid. He compiled a notebook of *Scripture Confirmations* and documented his text with frequent quotations from the Epistles. That is noteworthy, because he had previously regarded them as non-canonical and cited them only sparingly. He also made significant and affirmative use of the traditional creeds.

Further, the work is organized around Lutheran theological constructs, following the pattern of traditional Lutheran systematic theologies more than the structure of his own thought. For example, Swedenborg's theology would not have prompted separate chapters on the three persons of the Trinity or a chapter on imputation, and presumably would have prompted chapters on heaven and hell, providence, and marriage. In short, the work seems best understood not as a final summary of his theology but as a demonstration that his theology was "truly Christian" and a proposal for the rethinking of Lutheran theology. In a way, it tries to bridge the gap between the universalizing metaphysical concepts of *Divine Love and Wisdom* and traditional Christian beliefs, which are often interpreted with a severe parochialism. Swedenborg demonstrates that the encounter with the transcendent requires a complete rethinking of orthodox concepts, not necessarily contradicting them verbally, but seeing radically new meaning in familiar words.

The attacks on Swedenborg's work and reputation through his friends eventually became so troublesome that he appealed to King Adolph Fredrik, husband of Queen Louisa Ulrika who had been impressed by Swedenborg's clairvoyance. He complained that Beyer and Rosen—and, indeed, his own works—had "become, to a certain extent, martyrs, at least so far as regards the cruel persecutions by the bishop and the dean of that town . . . [through] sheer invectives, which do not contain a particle of truth."[32] After one decree of condemnation, the Royal Council recommended clement treatment of the offenders, and after further appeal, the case was dropped with no official verdict.

Before the legal wheels had finished grinding, however, Swedenborg had finished the first draft of *True Christian Religion,* and immediately thereafter experienced perhaps the most dramatic spiritual experience of his life. Transported into spiritual realms, he tells us, he found himself a witness to a gathering of the twelve apostles who had followed the Lord on earth. He heard the Lord himself announce the establishment of a new religious era, and saw the apostles sent to bear news of it to the whole spiritual world. He witnessed this on June 19, 1770, a date he regarded as marking the beginning of new spiritual possibilities for the human race.

Final Journey

In July 1770, Swedenborg sailed from Sweden for the eleventh time, stopping in Copenhagen to visit with a long-time friend, General Tuxen, and proceeding to Amsterdam with his manuscript of *True Christian Religion* for publication.

The following August, now eighty-three years old, he returned to London. He had several good friends there: an Anglican priest, the Rev. Thomas Hartley, Rector of Winwick; a physician, Dr. Husband Messiter; and a Quaker businessman, William Cookworthy. Hartley had heard of the accusations of heresy in Sweden, and had offered asylum should Swedenborg need it (although in fact, he had been in no personal danger).

Swedenborg took lodgings with a London wigmaker, Richard Shearsmith, and continued his meditations and his work on *The Coronis* (Appendix) *to True Christian Religion* included in *Posthumous Theological Works.* He kept at his manuscripts, working at all hours of the day and night, and often was heard speaking aloud—apparently to the spirits who appeared in his visions. Shortly before Christmas 1771, he suffered a stroke, but within a month he had partially recovered his speech, and resumed his writing.

Shearsmith's maid (who subsequently became Mrs. Shearsmith) described Swedenborg as a pleasant tenant, friendly to her. She tells how he predicted the day and time of his death, saying that "he was pleased . . . as if he were going to have a holiday."[33] She also reports that on Sunday, March 29, 1772, she was sitting at his bedside when he asked the time. When she told him it was five o'clock, he replied that that was good. He thanked her and blessed her, "and about ten minutes after, he heaved a gentle sigh, and expired in the most tranquil manner."[34]

In the latter part of his life, Swedenborg had maintained more active contact with the angels of his spiritual experiences than with the congregations and sermons of his father's church; but about a fortnight before his death, he had requested and received Holy Communion in his room from the Reverend Arvid Ferelius, pastor of the Swedish church in London. Ferelius also conducted Swedenborg's funeral in the Swedish church on Princes Square at four o'clock on Sunday, April 5, 1772. The service was well attended, filling the small church. The body was laid to rest under the altar. In Sweden, a eulogy was read in the House of Nobles by Samuel Sandels, Councillor of Mines.

In 1908, when London's Swedish church was threatened with demolition, the Royal Swedish Academy of Sciences arranged to have Swedenborg's casket brought home to Sweden lying in state on the deck of the Swedish warship *Fylgia*. The ship sailed from England on April 7. On May 18, the body was laid to rest in Uppsala Cathedral, burial place of King Gustavus Vasa and other Swedish monarchs. Swedenborg's sarcophagus is in a side chapel next to the tomb of Carolus Linnaeus.

The Dilemma
Resolved

To summarize Swedenborg's career as a theological writer, we begin with an individual profoundly committed both to a Lutheran view of the exclusive centrality of Scripture and to the spirit of open, empirical inquiry with its insistence that truth was everywhere to be found by the honestly inquiring mind. We find the tension between these commitments driving him to one discovery after another, each new step disclosing a further prospect. We find him encountering meaning in quite unexpected forms, particularly in direct, intense, and enlightening spiritual experience. We find a distinct tension at this level, issuing in uncertainty as to the best means of fulfilling his mission. As his two commitments blend into one, this uncertainty is resolved by a kind of alternation between exegetical, experiential, and topical presentation; and in this alternation we can see the interactive effects of his divine mandates, his own conscious judgment, his deeper sense of urgency, and his circumstances.

Three years before his death, Swedenborg responded to a request by his English friend, the Reverend Thomas Hartley, giving some biographical details of his life. After listing many of his honors, professional positions, and connections, he wrote:

But all that I have thus far related, I consider of little

importance; for it is far exceeded by the circumstance, that I have been called to a holy office by the Lord Himself, who most graciously appeared to me, ... opened my sight into the spiritual world, and enabled me to converse with spirits and angels, in which state I have continued up to the present day.[35]

Certainly that "circumstance" dominated the final third of his life more completely than any other influence. Nevertheless, the learning, the attitudes, and the methods of working developed over the course of the author's first fifty-six years affected his understanding and his way of communicating his divine revelation; and acquaintance with those characteristics contributes to our understanding of his theological works.

The interplay between his early life and his later revelation can be seen with particular poignancy in a passage from *True Christian Religion* (paragraph 508). Describing a temple seen in heaven during one of his spiritual experiences, he wrote: "I saw written over the gate: `Now it is permitted'; and this meant that permission now is granted to enter with discernment into the mysteries of faith." The searcher had reached his goal. The struggle between competing claims of faith and scientific discernment, which had engaged him for seventy years—his father and his church on one side, his "second father" and his university on the other—finally had come to resolution. Led by divine revelation, the engineer–legislator–administrator–scientist–theologian at last had found a place where science and religion were one.

Key Concepts in Swedenborg's Theology

In paragraph 172 of his last published work, *True Christian Religion*, Swedenborg wrote, "Anyone who reads the Athanasian Creed with open eyes can see that nothing less than a trinity of gods was understood by the participants in the Council of Nicea, who brought forth that creed like a stillborn infant." Yet beginning at paragraph 55 of an earlier work, *The Doctrine of the Lord*, he had written "that the import of the Athanasian faith is in accord with the truth, if only we understand the `trinity of persons' to mean the trinity of person that exists in the Lord." This contrast between scorn for Nicean "tritheism" and acceptance of a truth behind the formulation may serve to suggest the subtlety of the difference between Swedenborg's theology and traditional Christian theology; and the contrast may also serve to introduce two of his key concepts as underlying the others.

In regard to the subtlety, Swedenborg was well aware of the limitations of language. If his expositions sometimes seem to proceed at a snail's pace by reason of repetitiveness, this may be ascribed to a sense of need to carry his context with him. It bears witness also to his strong sense of the relatedness of all his concepts, to his love of detail, and to his insistence on looking at everything from all sides. Theology could not be reduced to a tidy system of dry, precisely defined terms. It had to be explored and loved and lived.

Two broad key concepts may help define the subtlety. The first is the concept of *distinguishable oneness.* For example, while the form and the substance of an object can usefully be distinguished from each other, they cannot be separated from each other in actuality. In precisely similar fashion, Swedenborg held that love, wisdom, and action can usefully be distinguished from each other, but cannot be separated from each other in actuality. This principle he extended to all of reality, insisting that nothing exists in isolation, and particularly that the Divine is essentially one in the special sense that it is wholly present everywhere and always, in an infinite number of distinguishable forms.[36]

The second underlying key concept that may help define the subtlety is that of *the reality of spirit.* For Swedenborg, there is nothing vague or amorphous about spirit. It is substantial, crisp, clear, and potent. Angels are in human form, with marvelously acute senses, experiencing themselves and their environment as solid. By comparison, the physical world is cloudy, ambiguous, and sluggish.[37]

With these basic concepts in mind, then—distinguishable oneness and the reality of spirit—we may look at some more specific concepts.

God

God is the absolute "distinguishable One," both within and transcending all space and all time, by nature incapable of being less than wholly present. The fundamental nature of the universe is therefore coherent at all times and in all places: the same fundamental laws apply everywhere, as indeed science assumes, either intuitively or of necessity.[38]

To help us grasp the nature of that infinite oneness, we may distinguish the primary features of infinite love, wisdom, and power—love being ineffective without wisdom, wisdom inert without love, and power the wholly natural result of their oneness. God is one in the essential sense that there is no conflict within the Divine: love does not bid one course of action, with wisdom counseling another. This is a *qualitative* monotheism, not simply a numerical one.[39]

Love is intrinsically personal, and God is therefore the essential and only person, the definition of the human person. There is no other source of life, which is in its essence love. We have been created not "out of nothing," but quite literally "out of love," since love is by nature self-giving and self-expressive. We are in that sense differentiated from the Divine but never separated (again "distinguishably one"); we are recipients of being rather than beings. We differ from each other not in the presence of the Divine within us, but in our acceptance of or receptivity to the Divine.[40]

Our Humanity

Most of the time, however, we do not experience ourselves primarily as receptors of the Divine. We feel self-contained and self-sustaining. This appearance is God's intentional gift of freedom and rationality, which are designed to enable us to accept the Divine willingly and which therefore are capable of being used to reject it.[41]

The physical world is the arena in which we choose to accept or to reject. Its ambiguity is essential to this purpose, enabling us to convince ourselves that we are self-sustaining in fact, to focus on our distinguishability to the exclusion of our oneness. If we so choose, we voluntarily forfeit the unitive power of love and wisdom and thereby set ourselves against the fundamental nature of reality itself.[42] This rejection manifests itself in isolation and hostility, both internal and external. That is, we develop a delight in conflict with others, and our own loves and thoughts are in conflict with each other. Our satisfaction comes only at the expense of others, which is inherently unworkable.[43]

Love

Swedenborg sees love as the fundamental energy and substance of all human beings, with wisdom as its means.[44] Ultimately, we will believe what we want ("love") to believe and understand what we want to understand. Our purposes, rather than our knowledge, determine our character—we *are* our love.[45]

Swedenborg distinguishes a hierarchy of loves: love of God as the Lord, love of others, love of the world, and love of self. All are necessary, and when they are in this order of priority, all are good. Love of self (or of the world) becomes harmful only when it dominates the higher loves rather than serving them. In practical terms, this means that Swedenborgian theology provides no warrant for asceticism or "renunciation of the world," but rather calls us to care for our own well-being, and values all moments of genuine joy, whether physical or spiritual.[46]

This affirmative stance is particularly clear in his treatment of marriage. He sees marriage as offering an opportunity for the most complete uniting of love and wisdom, so that the fully married couple is "distinguishably one" with no hint of domination by either of the other.[47] As the two become more and more one, each becomes more perfectly defined—the husband more a man, the wife more a woman.

Human Process

From birth, we have moments of spontaneous empathy, but the more dominant mode of our sensitivity seems to be self-sensitivity. This entails a radically distorted view of reality, giving each individual the impression of being the only one with live feelings and thoughts. Our egocentricity has an Achilles' heel that is specifically vulnerable to rationality because the thought that one is the only such being is rationally absurd.[48]

A further consequence of this is that our feeling and our thought—our "love" and our "wisdom"—unlike God's, are often in conflict. Sometimes, for example, we can see mentally what is good even when we do not feel it, and we have the freedom to follow that sight rather than the feelings. To the extent that we do so, we gradually become conscious of our latent "other-sensitivity." In one of Swedenborg's images, we open the way for the Lord's presence within us to flow through into our consciousness. This results in increasing "oneness" within us as well as with others.[49]

It must be stressed that this process of growth requires an active life in the world. The primary agent of change is constructive activity; and the disciplines of private study, self-examination, or meditation are effective only as they focus on such activity. Again, this is consistent with Swedenborg's emphasis on wholeness: the individual is not fulfilled by neglecting an entire level of being.[50]

Revelation

It is axiomatic for Swedenborg that we cannot lift ourselves by our own bootstraps. If it seems that we can, it is because God is constantly providing us with the resources for change. In Swedenborg's thought, rationality is a primary agent in this change, revelation is a primary form of divine aid, and the Bible is the central revelation. He finds the Bible to be essentially a parable, a literal story embodying a spiritual one. This conviction was so strong that he regarded the heart of his mission as the disclosing of the spiritual meaning of Scripture.[51]

He came to see the Bible not as a compendium of theological propositions or proof-texts, but as a coherent story. The process of growth noted under "Human Process" involves a lifelong task, which proceeds in an orderly fashion from more physical interests to more spiritual ones. The underlying order of that process is reflected in the biblical story under the primary image of the establishment of the kingdom of God. The literal story moves from an initial vague promise through many vicissitudes to the successful founding of an earthly empire. When this proves inadequate, the Incarnation translates the hope into one of a spiritual kingdom, the "kingdom of heaven," which is at last prophetically realized in the descent of the Holy City.[52]

In precisely analogous fashion, we can progress from our first vague childhood "dreams of glory" through experience to the establishment of self-identity; can realize the inadequacy of that outward appearance; and can become conscious participants in the vibrant world of spiritual love, wisdom, and activity.[53]

Correspondence

In the process of spiritual realization, the ambiguities of the world and of the Bible become increasingly resolved. The central concept in that resolution is the concept of "correspondence" or "responsiveness."[54] The Divine, as the source of all, works most directly through the spiritual realm into the physical; and while the divine nature is progressively obscured by the growing unresponsiveness of these successive realms, it is never obliterated.[55]

Swedenborg therefore sees the physical world as the result of spiritual causes, a result that reflects those causes, albeit dimly at times. The growth of deeper consciousness brings an understanding of this relationship. Laws of nature are seen as reflections of spiritual laws; physical entities and events are seen as results and therefore images of spiritual ones. The effort toward establishing an earthly kingdom is an appropriate prelude to the establishment of a heavenly one because the underlying principles are the same in each case. The instances are "distinguishable" in level, one being internal to the other, and "one" in principle.[56]

Universality

To refer for a moment to the first paragraph of these "Key Concepts," there is one respect in which the difference between Swedenborgian theology and traditional Christian theology emerges with no subtlety whatever. That is, Swedenborg insists that the Lord is *effectively* present in all religions, with the result that "the good individuals" of all religions are saved. He speaks far more affirmatively, in fact, about non-Christians than about Christians. For him, a god who did not provide at least the means of salvation to everyone must be unloving, unwise, or ineffective.[57]

Yet there is no hesitation in his insistence that the Incarnation of God in the person of Jesus was the turning point of all history, and that genuine Christianity is therefore the most perfect of all religions. Perhaps the most straightforward way to explain this apparent paradox is to state that in Christianity we see most clearly the God who is active everywhere. It is a distortion of that religion itself to claim that salvation is for Christians alone.[58]

Immortality

Seeing spirit as substantial and structured, Swedenborg sees people as essentially spiritual beings, whose bodies are primarily means of usefulness in a physical environment. For him, it is in fact preoccupation with the physical that blinds us to the reality of spirit. So on the one hand, progress toward oneness entails growing spiritual awareness, and on the other, death results primarily in a shift in the level of consciousness.[59]

The choice after death is not necessarily instantaneous. Swedenborg describes a "World of Spirits" between heaven and hell,[60] where the newly deceased gradually lose their ability to dissemble, and resolve any remaining indecisions. The only "judgment" we experience is our own—our free choice to care for each other, which is heaven, or to care only for ourselves, which is is hell.[61]

Maximus Homo

Because the trinity of love, wisdom, and power is characteristic of the Divine, it is characteristic of all reality; and because that trinity is intensely personal, the human form is pervasive. Swedenborg sees it as the form of the individual almost as a matter of course. Further, any group of people united by mutual love and understanding will act as a collective individual, and will therefore have a functional human form (distinguishable from "human shape"). He even refers to heaven in its entirety as the *Maximus Homo*, the "greatest person" or "universal human," and goes into some detail about the spiritual functions corresponding to the various members and organs of the human body. The collective person needs to perceive and act, to ingest and incorporate, just as the individual does, and therefore needs the "organs" which perform these functions.[62]

Incarnation

As noted, Swedenborg regards the Incarnation as the central event of human history. In his view, the human race declined from a primal state of innocence, becoming progressively more materialistic, until the only way it could be reached was through the physical presence of deity. In the Christ, Swedenborg sees God as assuming our own fallen nature and transforming it by the process of conflict between the divine best and the human worst within him. This experience precisely parallels our own inner conflicts, and his life is therefore the model for our own.[63]

The virgin birth, in this understanding, is essential for two reasons. First, there must be a physical parent to transmit the fallen nature: for Swedenborg, an *immaculate conception*, conception by a sinless mother, would have been quite pointless and ineffective. Second, there needed to be within that fallen nature an *infinite* capacity for the acceptance of the Divine. Without the first, Jesus' life would have been irrelevant to ours; without the second, it would have failed in its purpose.[64]

Jesus is then seen as having grown as we do, knowing doubt, selfishness, and all the distortions of humanity we can experience in ourselves. His life is the perfect exemplar of the process of transformation which is our own hope, and which, as already noted, is imaged in the biblical story. He was in a very special sense "the Word made flesh" and the fulfillment of Scripture. The passion on the cross was not a sacrificial appeasement but a final trial, a final self-giving. By refusing to use miraculous means to override our rejection of him, Jesus took the last step into perfect, loving wholeness; and because that wholeness was complete, the resurrection included even his physical body.[65]

A Radical Claim

A central point of difference between Swedenborg's theology and traditional Christian thought, supported but hardly foretold by the concepts of his system, is his announcement that biblical prophesies of a Last Judgment and a Second Coming of the Lord had been fulfilled in his lifetime. He claims knowledge of these events on the authority of his having witnessed the judgment in the spiritual world, and interprets traditional concepts in their light. With the Last Judgment in 1757, as he sees it, the era symbolized by the "old" Christian church came to an end. The Second Coming—the return of the Lord after his resurrection and glorification described in the Gospels—ushers in a new Christianity and the establishment in 1770 of a new church in the spiritual world. He stated at one point that the church in the outward world would go on much as before, at least for a while, and he neither tried to found a new organization nor speculated on the form one might take. He expected instead that a new freedom of thought in spiritual matters would counter the dogmatism of traditional Christianity.[66]

A Vision

Swedenborg's theology is not just "brain faith," but a kind of program for the healing of individuals and of human society. It calls for the fullest development of the individual emotionally, intellectually, and behaviorally. It values open and profound love, clear and free thinking, and faithful activity. It relates these qualities directly to the nature of reality, thereby avoiding any system of arbitrary rewards and punishments. Above all, it points toward an individual and collective oneness in which differences are not divisive but consistently enrich the whole, and sees the source of this "distinguishable oneness" as the wisdom and love of the one creator.[67]

Notes

Publication information for all titles is included in the bibliography. Swedenborg numbered all his paragraphs, and references are to these numbers, rather than to pages. Paragraph numbers are uniform in all editions.

◆

1. Swedenborg, *Journal of Dreams*, no. 18.
2. Tafel, *Documents*, 1:208.
3. *Ibid.*, 1:107.
4. Acton, *Letters*, 2:696.
5. *Ibid.*, 2:696.
6. Swedenborg, *Spiritual Diary*, nos. 3317, 3464.
7. Consciously, at least, Jesper did not intend to lead his sons away from their natural interests and toward ministry (see Tafel, *Documents*, I:196); but at age 56, Emanuel's dream suggests that he sensed his father's approval only after his own theophany (see note 16).
8. Tafel, *Op. cit.* 2:3.
9. *Ibid.*, 1:224.
10. Acton, *Op. cit.*, 1:56ff.
11. Models of Emanuel's airplane have been constructed for display in the Tekniska Museum in Stockholm, the Smithsonian Institution in Washington, D.C., and for the Swedenborg Foundation's travelling museum exhibit, "Swedenborg, Scientist."
12. *Daedalus Hyperboreus IV*, cited in Söderberg, *Swedenborg's 1714 Airplane.*
13. Tafel, *Op. cit.*, 1:305.
14. Swedenborg, *Economy*, no. 19; Swedenborg, *Spiritual Diary*, no. 2951.
15. Tafel, *Documents*, 1:586–90.
16. Swedenborg, *Economy*, no. 18.
17. Anders Johan, Count von Hopken, was a member (1746–1761) of the

Executive Council that shared power with the king of Sweden. Von Hopken later claimed to have been a friend of Swedenborg's for forty-two years and a daily companion since 1756. The president of the House of Nobles at this time was Count Carl Gustaf Tessin, an architect who had completed the Royal Palace in Stockholm (begun by his father, Nicolas Tessin) and who subsequently became a member for twenty years of the Executive Council. Tessin and Swedenborg knew each other in government service during these years, and in 1760—after Tessin learned that Swedenborg was the author of the theological works that were causing a stir in Stockholm—the two men held long private conversations about Swedenborg's philosophical and theological positions.

18. Swedenborg, *Journal of Dreams*, nos. 38–49.
19. *Ibid.*, nos. 49–57.
20. *Ibid.* nos. 58–59. (see also Note 7)
21. Tafel, *Op. cit.*, 2:709ff.
22. This description of the event conflates two accounts of Swedenborg's recollections preserved by his friends—one by Carl Robsahm (Tafel, *Documents*, 1:36), and the other by Gabriel Beyer (Tafel, *Documents*, 2:426). Swedenborg's *Spiritual Diary*, no. 397, apparently refers to a nightmarish self-abnegation related to this event.
23. Swedenborg, *True Christian Religion*, no. 779 and elsewhere.
24. Tafel, *Op. cit.*, 2:652.
25. Among them: the Last Judgment (1757) so changed the spiritual situation that a new approach was needed; he changed his focus from the generalized universal church to his particular vision of a new church; and even that the length of the work was making it prohibitively expensive to publish!
26. The difference between the two is explained in detail in Chapter V of William F. Wunsch, *The World within the Bible*.
27. Swedenborg, *Conjugial Love*, no. 521ff.
28. Kant, *Dreams of a Spirit-Seer*, 162.
29. See Robert H. Kirven, "Swedenborg and Kant" in *Swedenborg and His Influence*.
30. Sigstedt, *Swedenborg Epic*, 324. The consistories were regional courts of clergy, appointed to regulate ecclesiastical affairs.
31. Tafel, *Op. cit.*, 2:306.
32. *Ibid.*, 2:377.
33. *Ibid.*, 2:546.
34. *Ibid.*, 2:600.
35. *Ibid.*, 1:8–9.

Notes to Key Concepts (pp. 65–74)

36. Swedenborg, *Divine Love and Wisdom,* nos. 14, 77–81.
37. ———, *Arcana Coelestia,* nos. 6724, 7270; *Divine Love and Wisdom* 40.
38. ———, *Divine Love and Wisdom,* nos. 23, 27.
39. *Ibid.,* no. 28.
40. *Ibid.,* no. 11, 4, 78.
41. ———, *Marriage Love,* no. 444; *Divine Love and Wisdom,* no. 264.
42. ———, *Heaven and Hell,* no. 547ff.
43. *Ibid.,* no. 550.
44. ———, *Arcana Coelestia,* no. 6135(3).
45. ———, *Divine Providence,* no. 195(2); *Divine Love and Wisdom,* nos. 40ff.
46. ———, *Heaven and Hell* no. 528.
47. ———, *Arcana Coelestia,* nos. 10168–75.
48. *Ibid.,* no. 6323.
49. *Ibid.,* no. 2694(2).
50. ———, *Heaven and Hell,* no. 475.
51. ———, *Arcana Coelestia,* nos. 64, 67–9, 10632(4).
52. *Ibid.,* no. 3304(3).
53. *Ibid.,* nos. 69, 92.
54. *Ibid.,* no. 3769.
55. *Ibid.,* no. 3223.
56. *Ibid.,* no. 5173(2), *Heaven and Hell,* no. 406.
57. ———, *Divine Providence,* no. 326(9)ff.
58. *Ibid.,* no. 322(4)f.
59. ———, *Arcana Coelestia,* no. 8939(2).
60. ———, *Heaven and Hell,* no. 421ff.
61. *Ibid.,* no. 499ff.
62. ———, *Arcana Coelestia,* no. 4302(3). For a comprehensive discussion, see *Arcana* excerpts collected in Swedenborg, *The Universal Human.*
63. *Ibid.,* no. 3061(2).
64. *Ibid.,* no. 2288.
65. ———, *True Christian Religion,* no. 109.
66. ———, *Last Judgment,* nos. 73–74.
67. ———, *Arcana Coelestia,* no. 9613, *Last Judgment,* no. 12.

Bibliography

Titles are listed in the short form which appears in the notes and index, followed by original original title, published English title (and in some cases, an alternative translation), and place and date of first publication. English versions of works by Swedenborg are kept in print with various publication dates by the Swedenborg Foundation. Further publication details, and various translations and editions, can be found in Woofenden, *Swedenborg Researcher's Manual*.

Works by Emanuel Swedenborg

Animal Kingdom. *Oeconomia Regni Animalis (Economy of the Animal Kingdom [Dynamics of the Soul's Domain].* Amsterdam: 1741.

Apocalypse Explained. *Apocalypsis Explicata (Apocalypse Explained).* Unpublished by Swedenborg. Autograph manuscript in library of the Royal Academy of Sciences, Stockholm.

Apocalypse Revealed. *Apocalypsis Revelata (Apocalypse Revealed).* Amsterdam: 1766.

Arcana Coelestia. *Arcana Coelestia (Heavenly Mysteries).* London: 1749-1756.

Balance of Trade. *Copia af en instruction . . . [etc.]* (Titled by Tafel, in *Documents*, as "On the Means to further the Welfare of a country." Copy in the Diocesan Library, Linköping.

Brief Exposition. *Summaria Expositio Doctrinae Novae Ecclesiae (Brief Exposition of the Doctrines of the New Church).* Amsterdam: 1769. Autograph manuscript in Royal Academy of Sciences, Stockholm.

Continuation. *Continuatio de Ultimo Judico (Continuation concerning the Last Judgment).* Amsterdam: 1763.

Copper and Brass. *Regnum subterraneum sive minerale du cupro et orichalco (Subterranean or mineral kingdom in respect to copper and brass).* Vol. 3 of *Philosophical and Mineralogical Works,* Leipzig: Friedrich Hekel, 1743.

Coronis. *Coronis seu appendix ad Veram Christianam Religionem (Coronis to True Christian Religion).* Unpublished by Swedenborg. Manuscript in library of the Swedenborg Society, London. In *Posthumous Theological Works*. Ed. and trans. John Whitehead. New York: Swedenborg Foundation, 1928.

Daedalus. *Daedalus Hyperboraeus (Northern Inventor).* Journal in six issues, Emanuel Swedenborg, editor and contributor. Various places of publication, October 23, 1715–October 1718.

Divine Love and Wisdom. *Sapientia angelica de Divino Amore et de Divina Sapientia (Angelic Wisdom concerning Divine Love and Wisdom).* Amsterdam: 1763.

Divine Providence. *Sapientia angelica de Divina Providentia (Angelic Wisdom concerning Divine Providence).* Amsterdam: 1764.

Doctrine of Faith. *Doctrina Novae Hierosolymae de Fide (Doctrine of Faith for the New Jerusalem).* Amsterdam: 1763.

Doctrine of Life. *Doctrina Vitae pro Nova Hierosolyma (Doctrine of Life for the New Jerusalem).* Amsterdam: 1763.

Doctrine of Sacred Scripture. *Doctrina Novae Hierosolymae de Scriptura Sacra (Doctrine of the New Jerusalem concerning Sacred Scripture).* Amsterdam 1763.

Doctrine of the Lord. *Doctrina Novae Herosolymae de Domino (Doctrine of the New Jerusalem concerning the Lord).* Amsterdam: 1763.

"Dynamics of the Soul's Domain" (See *Economy of the Animal Kingdom*)

Earths in the Universe. *De Telluribus in Mundo nostro Solari (Earths in our Solar System [Earths in the Universe]).* London:1758.

Economy of the Animal Kingdom. *Oeconomia regni animalis (Economy of the Animal Kingdom [Dynamics of the Soul's Domain]).* Amsterdam: Francois Changuion, 1741.

Festivus Applausus. *Festivus Applausus in Caroli XII (Jovial Applause for Charles XII).* Greifswalde: Dan. Benj. Starkii, 1714.

First Principles of Natural Things (See *Principia*).

Four Doctrines. (See *Doctrine of Faith, Doctrine of Life, Doctrine of Sacred Scripture, Doctrine of the Lord*).

Heaven and Hell. *De Caelo et ejus mirabilibus, et de inferno, ex auditis et visis (Heaven and Its Wonders, and Hell, from Things Heard and Seen).* London: 1758.

"Heavenly Mysteries" (See *Arcana Coelestia*).

Inflation and Deflation. *Oförgripeliga tanckar om swenska myntets förhögning oest (Modest thoughts on the Deflation and Inflation of Swedish Coinage).* Stockholm: Joh. Hinr. Werner, 1722.

Intercourse between Soul and Body. *De Commercio Animae et Corporis (Soul-Body Interaction [Intercourse between Soul and Body]).* London: 1769.

Iron and Steel. *Regnum subterraneum sive minerale de ferro . . . deque conversione feri crude in chalybdem (Subterranean or mineral kingdom in respect to iron . . . further the method of converting crude iron into steel).* Vol. 2 of *Philosophical and Mineralogical Works*, Leipzig: Friedrich Hekel, 1743.

Journal of Dreams. *Swedenborgs Drömmar (Swedenborg's Dreams [Journal of Dreams]).* Unpublished by Swedenborg. Autograph manuscript in Royal Library, Stockholm.

Marriage Love. Delitiae sapientiae de Amore conjugiali (Delights of Wisdom pertaining to Conjugial [Marriage] Love). Amsterdam: 1768.

Maximus Homo. (See "Universal Human").

New Jerusalem and Its Heavenly Doctrine. De Nova Hierosolyma et ejus Doctrina coelesti (New Jerusalem and Its Heavenly Doctrine). London: 1758.

New Method of Finding Longitude. Försök at finna östra och westra lengden igen igenom manan (Attempt to find east and west longitude by means of the moon). Uppsala: J. H. Werner, 1718.

Noble and Base Metals. Swedenborg's Memorial, *Angaenda bearbetandet af jern och koppar i Sverige* (Swedenborg's *Proposition to abolish the distinction made in mining districts in favor of copper to the detriment of iron).* Copy in the State Archives, Stockholm.

On Tremulation. "Anatomi af var aldrafinaste natur, wisande att wart rörande och lefwande wäsende bestar af contremiscentier" (Anatomy of our most subtle nature, showing that our moving and living force consists of vibrations). *Daedalus Hyperboraeus (Northern Daedalus).* VI:10–14 (April–June 1719).

Philosophical and Mineralogical Works. Opera Philosophica et Mineralogica (Philosophical and Mineralogical Works). 3 volumes: *I. Principia (First Principles), II. Regnum . . . de ferro (Iron and Steel), III. Regnum . . . de cupro et orichalco (Copper and Iron).* Leipzig: Friedrich Hekel, 1734.

Posthumous Theological Works. Posthumous Theological Works. 2 Vols. Ed. and trans. John Whitehead. New York: Swedenborg Foundation, 1928. Includes other items listed herein.

Principles of Chemistry. Prodromus principiorum rerum naturalium (Forerunner of First Principles of Natural Things [Principles of Chemistry]). Amsterdam: Johannem Oosterwyk, 1721.

Scripture Confirmations. Dicta Probantia (Scripture Confirmations of New Church Doctrine, being proof passages from the Scriptures). Unpublished by Swedenborg. Ed. and trans. John Whitehead. New York: Swedenborg Foundation, 1914. Also in vol. 2 of *Posthumous Theological Works,* 1928.

Selected Sentences. L. Annaei Senecae & Pub. Syri Mimi forsnan & aliorum Selectae Sententiae (Selected Sentences from L. Annaeus Seneca and Publius Syrus the Mime with Notes, submitted by Emanuel Swedberg for public examination June 1, 1709 at Uppsala University). Uppsala: Uppsala University, 1709.

"Soul's Domain" (See *Animal Kingdom).*

Soul-Body Interaction. See *Intercourse between Soul and Body.*

Spiritual Diary. Diarium Spiritualis (Spiritual Diary). Unpublished by Swedenborg. Autograph manuscript in the Royal Academy of Sciences, Stockholm. *Spiritual Diary.* 5 Vols. Trans. George Bush and John Smithson. London: James Speirs, 1883–1902. Reprints by the Swedenborg Foundation, New York.

True Christian Religion. Vera Christiana Religio (True Christian Religion). Amsterdam: 1771

Universal Human. The Universal Human. (Extracts from *Arcana Coeles-tia).* Trans. George F. Dole. New York: The Paulist Press, 1984.

White Horse. De Equo Albo, de quo in Apocalypsi, cap xix (The White Horse Mentioned in the Apocalypse Chapter xix). London: 1758.

Word Explained. Explicatio in Verbum historium Veteris testament (The Historical Word of the Old Testament Explained). Unpublished by Swedenborg. Autograph manuscript in the Royal Academy of Sciences, Stockholm. *The Word of the Old Testament Explained.* 9 vols. Ed. and trans. Alfred Acton. Bryn Athyn, PA: 1928–51.

Worship and Love of God. De cultu et amore Dei (Worship and Love of God). London: 1745.

Works by Other Authors

Acton, Alfred, compiler, editor, and translator. *Letters and Memorials of Emanuel Swedenborg.* 2 vols. Bryn Athyn, PA: Swedenborg Scientific Association, 1948, 1955.

Brock, Erland. *et al,* eds. *Emanuel Swedenborg: The Man and His Influence.* Bryn Athyn, PA: Academy Press, 1989.

Larsen, Robin, ed. *Emanuel Swedenborg: A Continuing Vision.* New York: Swedenborg Foundation, 1988.

Sigstedt, Cyriel Odhner. *The Swedenborg Epic.* New York: Bookman, 1952.

Söderberg, Henry. *Swedenborg's 1714 Airplane: A Machine to Fly in the Air.* New York: Swedenborg Foundation, 1988.

Tafel, Rudolph H., compiler, editor, translator. *Documents Concerning the Life and Character of Emanuel Swedenborg.* 2 vols. (bound as 3). London: Swedenborg Society, 1875, 1877.

Toksvig, Signe. *Emanuel Swedenborg, Scientist and Mystic.* New Haven: Yale University Press, 1948.

Woofenden, William Ross. *Swedenborg Researcher's Manual: A Research Reference Manual for Writers of Academic Dissertations, and for Other Scholars.* Bryn Athyn, PA: Swedenborg Scientific Association, 1988.

Wunsch, William F. *The World within the Bible: A Handbook to Sweden-borg's Arcana Coelestia.* New York: New Church Press, 1929.

Illustration Sources

Unless otherwise noted, these images are from the Swedenborg Image Archive, at the offices of the Swedenborg Foundation, West Chester, Pennsylvania.

◆

Frontispiece.   Johann-Martin Bernigeroth. *Emanuel Swedenborg.* Engraving, 1734.

Title Page.   Ornament used in first printing of Swedenborg's *Philosophical and Mineralogical Works,* 1734.

Copyright page, iv.   Emanuel Swedenborg. *Outside View of a Finite Particle.* From *Principia.* Engraving, 1734.

Page vi.   Emanuel Swedenborg. Notes and sketch of his aircraft. Ink on paper, 1730. Teknisa Museet, Stockholm.

Page viii.   Count Erik Dahlberg. *View of Uppsala with the cathedral, the university, and the castle.* Engraving, 1716. Uppsala Universitetsbibliotek.

Page 3.   J. B. Busser. *Utkast till Beskrifning af Uppsala.* (Draft of a Description of Uppsala). Engraving, 1769. Uppsala Universitetsbibliotek.

Page 6.   Pehr Hilleström. *Miners at Work in the Falun Copper Mine.* Oil painting, 1781. Järnkontoret, Stockholm.

Pages 8 and 9.   Count Erik Dahlberg. Stockholm viewed from the west. From *Svecia Antiqua et Hodierna.* Engraving, 1716.

Page 11.   Unknown Artist. *Emanuel Swedenborg in his Nineteenth Year.* Oil painting, ca. 1707. Courtesy of the collection of Adolf Stroh.

Page 12.   Cindy Lippincott. Map of Swedenborg's first trip to the continent.

Page 14.   Unknown Artist. *A Bird's-Eye View of London.* Engraving, 18th century. British Museum, London.

Page 15.   Unknown Artist. *Octagon Room.* Engraving, 18th Century. Royal Greenwich Observatory, East Sussex.

Page 16. David Loggan. Bodleian Library in the Eighteenth Century. From *Oxania Illustrata*. Engraving, 1675. New York Public Library.

Page 17. S. and R. Larsen. Photograph of Swedenborg's microscope and case. 1983, by permission of Tekniska Museet, Stockholm.

Page 22. Swedenborg's Coat of Arms, 1719. Photograph collected by Virginia Branston.

Page 23. Count Erik Dahlberg. Riddarhuset. From *Svecia Antiqua et Hodierna*. Engraving, 1716.

Page 27. Autograph of Emanuel Swedenborg.

Page 29. Hoisting Machine. Engraving from Swedenborg's *Daedalus Hyperboreus*. Published by E. Swedenborg and Christopher Polhem. Stockholm, 1716. Courtesy of the Swedenborg Scientific Association. Photograph by Diane Fehon.

Page 30. Emanuel Swedenborg. The complete engraving *Evolution of the Planets*. From *Principia*, 1734.

Page 33. Adam or Gabrielle Perelle. *L'Observatoire Nationale*. Engraving, late 17th century.

Page 38. *Spiritual Diary*. Photolithograph. Swedenborg School of Religion Library, Newton, Massachusetts.

Page 41. Unknown Artist. *Swedenborg's Summerhouse*. Pen and Ink, 20th century. *Chrysalis: Journal of the Swedenborg Foundation* (1987) 2:155.

Pages 42 and 43. Harold T. Carswell, *Surmised Plan of Swedenborg's Property in Stockholm*. Ink on paper, 1922. *Chrysalis: Journal of the Swedenborg Foundation* (1987) 2:156.

Page 46. Count Erik Dahlberg. *Svecia antiqua et hodemia*. Engraving, mid-18th century.

Page 52. Pehr Hilleström. *Svindersvik*. Oil painting, late 18th century. Nordiska Museet, Stockholm.

Page 53. F. Birck. *Immanuel Kant*. Engraving, n.d. Bettman Archive, New York.

Page 56. Frontispiece from *Jerusalem*, by William Blake. Etching colored with watercolor, 1804–1820. Collection of Mr. and Mrs. Paul Mellon, Upperville, Virginia.

Emanuel Swedenborg Life Chronology

by Robert H. Kirven, *Proximus inter Aliis**

Born Emanuel Swedberg, January 29, 1688, at "Sveden," the ancestral homestead near Falun, the third of nine children, to:

Jesper Swedberg (born 28 August 1653)

    ordained 12 Feb 1682, chaplain of horse guards

    chaplain of court, 1685

    dean and pastor of Wingaker, Sodermanland, 1692

    dean of Uppsala Cathedral, 1694

    Superintendent of Swedish churches in America, London, and Portugal, 1696

    Bishop of Skara 1702 (lived at Brunsbo)

    Doctor of Theology, 1705

    Died July 7, 1735 at Brunsbo

and **Sara Behm** (12 December 1683–17 June 1696)

    Albrecht 1684–1696,

    Anna, 1686–1766,

    Emanuel, 1688–1772,

    Hedwig, 1690–1728,

    Danie1, 1691–1691,

    Eliezer 1691–1716

    Catharina, 1693–1770

    Jesper, 1694–1771

    Margareta, 1695–[?]

2 February 1688—Emanuel baptized at Jacob's Church, Stockholm

---

* Marguerite Beck Block began compiling this chronology, passing the work on to Virginia Branston, who turned it over to Robin Larsen. The present compiler received it from her and has profited from suggestions by his colleagues and students.

1692—Jesper becomes professor of theology at Uppsala, then rector of cathedral there

1692—beginning of Swedenborg's (later memory of) being constantly engrossed with "thoughts of God, salvation, and the spiritual diseases of men"

1696—Johan Moraeus, Emanuel's cousin, appointed as his tutor

17 June 1696—Sara Behm dies

1697—Charles XI dies, Charles XII (age 15) succeeds ("Lion of the North")

30 November 1697—Jesper marries Sara Bergia (born 4 Jan 1666)

15 June 1699—matriculates at Uppsala; joins Westmanland Dalecarlian Nation (fraternity); studies philosophy

1700—beginning of Swedenborg's (later memory of) "delight in conversing with clergymen about faith," and first experiments with hypoventilation

November 1700—Charles XII invades Ukraine

17 May 1702—fire at Uppsala; Prof. Rudbeck saves library

Spring 1703—Jesper and Sara Bergia move to Brunsbo, his home while bishop of Skara

18 July 1703—Anna Swedberg marries Eric Benzelius, born 27 January 1675

librarian and later professor of theology at Uppsala

1726—bishop of Gotenborg

1731— bishop of Linköping

Swedenborg lives with Eric and Anna (as well as Hedwig and two brothers) for six years

June 1709—Swedenborg is graduated from Uppsala

1709–1710—Swedenborg assembles fossil bones of whale

May 1710—**First Trip to the Continent**

3 August 1710—London

visited by cousins Andreas and Gustav Hesselius

reads Newton, Malebranche, Norris

performs Boyle's experiments

studies with Flamsteed

April 1711—computes tables for latitude of Uppsala, and solar and lunar eclipses from 1712–1721

16 January 1712—to Oxford

studies with Halley

studies Dryden, Spenser, Milton, Shakespeare, Jonson

writes poetry

early 1713—to Utrecht and Leyden

meets Swedish Ambassador, Count Carl Gyllenborg

meets Swedish Ambassador diplomat and mathematician, Baron Palmquist

meets Swedish British Ambassador Robinson

May 1713—Paris and Versailles

May 1714—Hamburg

July 1714—Rostock: finishes drawings of fourteen inventions: a submarine, a new kind of siphon, a weight lifter, a design for a sluice, a machine to throw out water, a drawbridge, an air pump (condenser-exhauster), air gun, a universal musical instrument, a technique for drawing in perspective, a water clock, a mechanical carriage, a flying carriage, cords, and springs

November 1714—Charles XII returns from Turkey; Swedenborg writes *Festivus Applausus*

June 1715—home to Brunsbo, Sweden

Christmas 1715—spends holiday with Benzelius at Starbo

January 1716—publishes first of six issues of *Daedalus Hyperboraeus*
   1st issue: ear trumpets and tubes;
   2nd: hoisting machine, coinage, solar eclipse;
   3rd: weights and measures, air pumps, air measurements;
   4th: flying machine (controllable glider)

January 1716—first visit to Polhem in Stiernsund

June 1716—Eliezer Swedberg dies (Swedenborg's younger brother)

September 1716—Christopher Polhem authorized to build dry dock at Karlscrona, E.S. accompanies;

December 1716—E.S. meets Charles XII at Lund; appointed extraordinary assessor, Board of Mines, by Charles XII; gets second appointment, but not paid or accepted by board

January 1717—joins Polhem in Karlscrona

April 1717—takes seat on Board of Mines, not allowed to sign documents

June 1717—writes proposal for instituting an observatory

1718—Swedenborg works on Gota Canal, inland waterway, saltworks, moves ships overland to siege of Frederickshald

21 January 1718—declines opportunity to succeed Professor Pehr Elfvius (mathematics) on Uppsala faculty

July 1718—reputed engagement between Swedenborg and Emerentia Polhem—Swedenborg was eventually rejected

November 1718—Swedenborg avoids fighting in campaign against Frederickshald

30 November 1718—Charles XII killed before Frederickshald,
   Ulrica Eleonora (1688–1741), younger sister of Charles XII and wife of Frederic, Crown Prince of Hesse–Cassel (1676–1751), claims throne of Sweden

1719—Swedenborg publishes *Motion and Position of Earth and Planets*

1719—Swedenborg publishes *The Height of the Waters, and Strong Tides in the Primaeval World*

1719—Swedenborg publishes *On Tremulation*

3 March 1719—Sara Bergia dies

17 March 1719—Ulrica Eleonora crowned
(renounced absolute monarchy before being ratified as queen by Cabinet and Diet; displaced claim to throne of her nephew, Charles Frederic, son of Charles XI's first daughter, Hedwig Sophia)

26 May 1719—Ulrica Eleonora ennobles Swedberg family; name changed to Swedenborg; Swedenborg seated in House of Nobles

Summer 1719—Swedenborg works on blast furnaces and airtight stoves

1720—Ulrica Eleonora's husband Frederic acknowledged by Diet as king of Sweden

May 1720—**Second European Trip**

> Leaves Starbo—Amsterdam, Leiden, Aix-la-Chapelles, Liege

> 1721—publishes *Prodromus Principium Rerum Naturalium (Principles of Chemistry)*

> 21 May 1721—Sara Bergia's estate divided: Starbo sold, proceeds divided: one-fifth split between Swedenborg and Lars Benzelstierna; four-fifths to Emanuel Swedenborg's aunt, Brita Behm. Swedenborg's share: 4,571 dalers

> 1722—Swedenborg leaves for Cologne, Leipzig;
> *Prodromus* favorably reviewed in *Acta Eruditorum*

> April 1722—Returns to Sweden
> Meets King Fredrick and Queen Eleonora at Medevi

July 1722—Returns to Stockholm

November 1722—Swedenborg publishes *Modest Thoughts on the Fall and Rise of Swedish Money*, a pamphlet against debasement of currency; presented to Riksdag

1723—Consistory of Uppsala University invites Swedenborg to apply for professorship, to succeed Nils Celsius; Swedenborg declines

February 1723—E.S. presents memorial, *The Balance of Trade to Riksdag Committee on Commerce and On Noble and Base Metals* to Committee on Mines

March 1723—Board of Mines seats E.S. as extraordinary assessor

1724—lawsuit with aunt Brita Behm over Axmar mines

1724—Swedenborg seeks to restore Polhem's models, stored at the College of Mines, for a Museum of Technology at Stockholm and a Museum of Mining at Falun

May 1724—E.S. visits with Jesper Swedenborg and Andreas Hesselius, returned from America; visits with Eric and Anna Benzelius; attends meeting of Uppsala Literary Society

15 July 1724—Board of Mines grants E.S. a salary of 800 dalers. Begins regular employment in Board of Mines

1725—Swedenborg takes nephew Eric Benzelius under his wing; instructs in physics and mathematics

1726—Swedenborg courts Stina Maja Steuchius—refused

1728—Hedwig dies

Swedenborg moves to apartment at Stora Nygatan for five years

1729—completes *The Lesser Principia*

18 March 1729—J. Unge (brother-in-law) urges Swedenborg to seek hand of Sebastian Tham's youngest daughter15 July 1724—Swedenborg appointed full assessor of Board of Mines, at salary of 1200 dalers

17 December 1729—St. Petersburg Academy of Sciences invites Swedenborg to become a member

1733—Brother-in-law Eric Benzelius becomes bishop of Linköping

May 1733—**Third European Trip**

    25 May—Stralsund

    27 May—Greifswalde

    28 May—Neu Brandenburg

    30 May—Old Strelitz

    2 June—Berlin

    7 June—Dresden

    20 June—finishes *Principia*

    23 July—Prague

    19 August—Prague

    30 August—Carlsbad

    3 September—Leipzig publishes *Principia*

    1733—comments on Wolff's *Cosmology* (cf. Woofenden, *Manual,* pp 37–38)

    1734—publishes *Opera Philosophica et Mineralia* (I. *Principia;* II. *On Iron and Steel;* III. *On Copper and Brass).* Favorably reviewed in *Acta Eruditorum*

Spring 1734—returns to Sweden

3 July 1734—attends Board of Mines

1735—publishes *On the Infinite*

July 1735—Bishop Swedberg dies

29 January 1736—Bishop Swedberg's funeral in Wästergötthland

July 1736—**Fourth European Trip**

    17 July 1736—departs for Copenhagen, Amsterdam, Belgium, Rotterdam

    In Amsterdam, meditates and sees "flashes of light"

    3 September—Paris

Studies with Winslow (Danish anatomist)

Visits Luxembourg Gardens, Notre Dame, Saint Chapelle

Lives in Rue de l'Observatoire

1738—writes *The Cerebrum*

Visits Burgundy, Turin, Mt. Cenis

12 March 1738—Italy

7 April 1738—leaves for Milan, Verona, Venice, Padua, and Florence

9 September 1738—arrives in Rome

13 February 1739—leaves for Genoa, Paris

May 1739—returns to Amsterdam

Again experiences "light influx"

Fall 1739—sends inlaid marble table home to Sweden

27 December—finishes *Oeconomia Regni Animalis* (influences from Leeuwenhoek, Malpighi, Ruysch, Bidloo, Booerhave, Descartes, Haller)

September 1740—The Hague

October 1740—to Denmark

Practices shallow breathing, experiences mysterious radiation

November 1740—returns to Stockholm

10 December 1740—Swedenborg accepted into Academy of Sciences with Anders von Hopken, Carl Linnaeus, Jonas Alstromer, Count Tessin

1740–1741—publishes *Oeconomia Regni Animalis*

1741—writes *The Fibre*

9 October 1741—moves into "Rantmasterehuset," n. 64 Slussen (second floor over coffee house)

1741–1742—influenced by Lappland shamans separating soul from body (the state of "ecstasy energumen")

1742—writes *Rational Psychology*

1743—Bishop Eric Benzelius dies (Swedenborg's brother-in-law)

26 March 1743—buys house in south Stockholm (Hornsgatan); sells shares in Starbo and Dalecarlian Ironworks to Count Gyllenborg

June 1743—takes leave from Board of Mines to write *Regnum Animale*

July 1743—Adolf Friedrich (m. Louisa Ulrika) elected successor to Swedish throne (1710–1771)

Fifth European Trip

21 July 1743—departs for Ystad, Pomerania, Hamburg, Bremen, Amsterdam, Leyden, The Hague

1743—writes *Hieroglyphic Key,* begins study of correspondences

1743–1744—publishes *The Brain in Amsterdam*

Records inner conflicts and dreams in *Journal of Dreams*

1744—The Hague: publishes *Regnum Animali,* vols. I and II

6 April 1744—in Delft, Vision of Christ

May 1744—London: lodges with Moravians

21 September 1744—first addressed by a spirit

October 1744—last entry in *Journal of Dreams* (except for one in May 1745)

1745—publishes Vol III of *Regnum Animali*

1745—composes Bible Index

1745—publishes Parts I and II of *Worship and Love of God*

April 1745, London—second Vision of Christ *(Spiritual Diary* Dec. 12, 1747, no. 397)

Spring 1745—returns to Stockholm; moves into home in Hornsgatan; when not travelling abroad lives and writes there for next twenty years

1746–1747—writes *Word Explained*

1746 or 1747—experiences automatic writing

1747–1756—writes *Spiritual Diary*

Spring 1747—Swedenborg offered post of Councillor of Mines

17 July 1747—resigns from Board of Mines

Sixth European Trip

18 June 1747—Holland

21 March 1748—experiences a death-like state while in Holland

September 1748—England; then to France for winter

December 1748–June 1756—writes *Arcana Coelestia*

1749–Joachim Wretman, Swedish merchant, becomes Swedenborg's agent

Summer 1749—printer John Lewis in London sells *Arcana,* vol. 1

Fall 1749—Aix-la-Chapelle for rest

15 October 1749—Stephen Penny applauds *Arcana*

Spring 1750—returns to Sweden, stays in Sodermalm near Lake Malar and Baltic Sea; begins gardening

1751—King Frederic dies; Adolf Frederick succeeds

1751—Countess Elizabeth Stierncrona Gyllenborg gives Swedenborg her manuscript (later, Swedenborg is said to have referred to her as his wife in spiritual world. She died in 1769)

1751—Swedenborg encounters in spiritual world (among others): Dr. Govan Norberg; Adam Leyel; Johan Bergenstierna; Johan Moraeus; Hans Bjorck; Charles XII; Anders Swab; Archbishop Jacob Benzelius; Bishop Rhydelius; Senator Sven Lagerberg; William Penn; Queen Christina (1626–1689; Q. of Sweden, 1632–1654; abdicated and converted to Catholicism); Saint Genevieve; Mary; Sara Behm

31 August 1751—Polhem dies

1755—Lars Benzelstierna dies

July 1756—ten conspirators to overthrow government executed; Louisa Ulrica forms Court Party, replacing Tessin with Count von Hopken as president of Council

Fall 1756—crop failure, famine, prohibition

September 1757—war declared between Sweden and Prussia (ends May 1762)

Summer 1758—**Seventh European Trip**

1758—London—Swedenborg writes and publishes *Earths in the Universe, The Last Judgment, New Jerusalem and Its Heavenly Doctrine, White Horse of the Apocalypse, Heaven and Hell*

5 January 1759—Count Gustav Bonde discovers Swedenborg is author of *Heaven and Hell* (Bonde is previous president of Board of Mines, senator, and chancellor of Uppsala).

June 1759—leaves England for home

19 July 1759—Vision of Stockholm fire, while E.S. is in Gothenburg at home of William Castel

1760—Daniel Tilas, minerologist, writes about Swedenborg's conversations with spirits

1760—Swedenborg attends Tessin's Saturday philosophy parties at Svindersvik

1760—writes tract on the Athanasian Creed

1760—Prelate Friedrich Christopher Oetinger, German scholar and writer, defends Swedenborg and himself against Consistory at Wurtemburg

1760—Ludwig IX wants to know how to converse with spirits

5 March 1760—former Prime Minister Carl Gustav Tessin visits Swedenborg

August 1760—Dr. Johann Ernesti, prof. of theology at Leipzig, criticizes Swedenborg's theological writings

November 1760—controversy with Anders Nordencrantz, councillor of Commerce, over foreign exchange

1761—Dr. Johan Rosen (professor) and Dr. Gabriel Andersson Beyer (teacher) favorably impressed with Swedenborg (later defend him)

1761—publishes *On Inlaying Tables*

February 1761—Count von Hopken forced to resign as prime minister: Political party "Caps" control government

Spring 1763—visited by Mr. Green (cf. Kant's letter to Frl. von Knobloch)

Spring 1763—**Eighth European Trip**

Travels to Amsterdam

1763—publishes *Four Doctrines*

1763—publishes *Divine Love and Divine Wisdom*

1764—publishes *Divine Providence*

1765—**Ninth European Trip**

1766—publishes *Apocalypse Revealed*

Spring 1766—London; presents *Method of Finding Longitude by the Moon to Royal Society of Sciences*

September 1766—returns to Stockholm

1766—Nicholas Collin (student of astronomy) meets Swedenborg; later becomes pastor of Swedish congregation in Pennsylvania and close friend of Benjamin Franklin

Tenth European Trip

27 May 1768—to Gothenburg and Holland

Publishes *Conjugial Love*

November 1768—meets John Christian Cuno, who makes thorough study of Swedenborg's teachings

Winter 1768–1769—in Sweden, beginning of opposition to Swedenborg. Controversy breaks out in Consistory over Swedenborg's teachings, pitting Bishop Lamberg and Dean Ekstrom against Drs. Beyer and Rosen; Dean Ekebom finds the doctrines abhorrent and heretical, and takes steps to prevent spread of Swedenborg's teachings, condemning them and accusing him of Socinianism

April 1769—to Paris

July 1769—to London

Thomas Cookworthy (druggist) and Rev. Thomas Hartley visit Swedenborg in London

Fall 1769—in Stockholm, Beyer and Rosen defend Swedenborg, telling Consistory to study his works before condemning them

Fall 1769—Swedenborg returns to Sweden

1769—Bishop Filenius argues against releasing fifty confiscated copies of *Conjugial Love*

1769—attempt to consign Swedenborg to asylum; friend in senate advises him to leave Sweden for safety; he declines

1769—publishes *A Brief Exposition of the Doctrines of the New Church, Soul-Body Interaction*

2 January 1770—Royal Council asks Consistory to report Swedenborg's errors to the king

April 1770—Royal Council can find nothing wrong with the doctrines and no longer wishes to publicize Swedenborgianism with controversy

Augustus and Claes Alstromer (brothers) in Department of Justice defend Beyer and Swedenborg

26 April 1770—Royal Council decrees "totally condemn, reject, and forbid" the theological doctrines in Swedenborg's writings. Beyer and

Rosen are condemned, advised to repent, and forbidden to teach theology. Confiscation of books ordered

25 May 1770—Swedenborg appeals to the king

19 June 1770—Founding of New Church in spiritual world

Eleventh European Trip

July 1770—Amsterdam

1771—publishes *True Christian Religion*

1771—King Adolphus Frederick dies; Gustav III succeeds

1771—Swedenborg publishes second pamphlet on currency, repeating and expanding his 1722 work

August 1771—to England

7 December 1771—in Stockholm, Royal Council says there is much that is true in Swedenborg's writings, and orders accused to be treated mildly

Beyer/Rosen case goes to Gotha Court of Appeals

Beyer/Rosen case goes to Uppsala University (case dropped in 1773)

Dec 1771—Swedenborg has stroke in England; partially recovers

1772—Swedenborg reaffirms his teachings, accepts communion from Rev. Arvid Ferelius

Sunday, 29 March 1772, 5 p.m.—Swedenborg dies (Drs. Hampe and Messiter attending physicians)

Sunday, 5 April 1772, 4 p.m.—Rev. Arvid Ferelius conducts funeral services

19 August 1772—Gustav III re-establishes absolute monarchy

7 October 1772—Councillor of Mines Samuel Sandels delivers eulogy in Great Hall of House of Nobles

1773—Rev. John Clowes of Manchester, England, becomes Swedenborgian

1778—Clowes establishes New Church Society among Anglican parishoners in Whitefield, near Manchester

5 December 1783—Robert Hindmarsh gathers first group of London Swedenborgians

31 July 1787—London group worships as separated church

1786—(Sweden) Exegetic and Philanthropic Society formed by Von Hopken, Charles Nordenskiold, and Charles Wadstrom to promote Swedenborg's doctrines.

Index

*Page numbers referring to illustrations are set in **bold** typeface.*

A

Aachen, 27
Adolph Fredrik, 58
airplane, 18
Aix-la-Chapelle, 27
Altenberg, 27
Amsterdam, 33–37, 61
anatomy, vii, 4, 35
angel(s), 44, 66
Aristotelianism, 5
Arndt, Johann, *True Christianity*, 9
Arrhusia, Christina, 25
astronomers, vii, 34
astronomy, 17, 28
Athanasian Creed, 65
Atlantis, 4
atomic theory, 31
Axmar, 25

B

Baltic Sea, 3
baptism, 8
Behm, Albrecht, 21
Behm, Brita, 25
Benzelius, Anna (Swedberg), 5, 7, 10, 33
Benzelius, Erik, 5, 10, 16, 19, 25, 28, 33
Benzelius, Erik, Jr., 28, 29
Benzelius, Lars, 25
Benzelstierna, Hedwig (Swedberg), 7, 25, 29
Benzelstierna, Lars, 25, 26
Berlin, 31
Beyer, Dr. Gabriel, 54, 55, 58
Bible, 5, 40, 42, 44, 50, 69, 70
Bible Index, 40, 41
"bible of Pietism," 9

Bidloo, Godfried, 33
Blake, William, *Jerusalem*, **56**
Board of Mines, 20, 21, 26–29, 31, 33, 34, 40, **46**, 50
Bodleian Library, **16**
Boerhaave, Hermann, 33
Bonde, Count Gustav, 50
Book of Revelation, 47
brain, 34–36, 44
"brain faith," 9, 74
brass-instrument making, 14, 17
breathing, minimal, 10, 34
Brunsbo, 10, 13, 25

C

cabinet making, 14
Cartesianism, 3, 4, 5
Castel, William, 48
Celsius, Nils, 28
Charles Frederick, 23
Charles XI, 3, 7–9, 13
Charles XII, 3, 13, 18, 19–21, 23–25, 40
chemistry, 14, 17, 29
childhood (of Swedenborg), 7–10
Christianity, 71
coat of arms, **22**
Cologne, 27
Consistory, Gothenburg, 54
constitutional limitations, 24
continent, **12**, 16
continuations, 49, 51
Cookworthy, William, 61
Copenhagen, 27, 33, 35, 61
Correspondence, 70–71
Council of the Realm, 24
criticism, 53–55
currency reform, 24, 28

D

Daedalus Hyperboreus, 19, 20
death, 72
death (of Swedenborg), 61–62
Denmark, 3, 13, 21
Descartes, Rene, vii, 3
diary, vii, 34, 35, **38**, 39, 42
dissection, 33, 34
dissertation, 11
distinguishable One, 66
distinguishable oneness, 66, 74
divine commission, 39–44, 52, 64
dream(s), vii, viii, 37, 39
Dresden, 31
drydock, 20, 21
ductless glands, 36

E

Easter, 37, 39
Ekebom, Dean Olaf, 55
England, 3, 4, 13, 16, 21, 48
　(see also London)
engraving, 14
Enlightenment, 3–5
ennoblement, 22, 24
Ernesti, Johann, 50, 51
Europe, 19, 20, 27, 31–33, 48
Evolution of the Planets, **30**
experience (spiritual), 39–44, 47,
　52, 59, 63, 64

F

Faith, viii, 5, 9, 10, 66
Falun, **6**, 7, 20, 21, 25, 28
father, 7–11, 32, 33, 39
Ferelius, Reverend Arvid, 62
fire, 4, 7, 14, 48
Flamsteed, John, viii, 15
flash [of light], 34
France, 13
Fredrik (king of Sweden), 23
Fredrikshald, 21
freedom, 67
Fylgia, Swedish warship, 62

G

geology, 32
geometry, 20
Germany, 3, 31, 50, 53
God, 44, 45, 66–67, 68–70, 73
Görtz, Baron George H. von, 23
Gothenburg, 48, 55

Great Copper Mountain (Stora
　Kopparberg), 7, 20
Gregorian calendar, 8
Gustav III, 25
Gyllenborg, Count Gustav Fredrik, 29

H

Hague, The, 27, 36, 37
Halley, Sir Edmund, 16
Hamburg, 27
Hartley, Reverend Thomas, 61, 63
Hebrew, 3
Hekel, Friedrich, 28
hoisting machine, **29**
hoists, 18
Hopken, Count Anders Johan von, 35
Hornsgatan (street), 29, 41
House of Clergy (Swedish), 24
House of Nobles (Swedish), **23**, 24, 62
Hudson, Dr. John, 16
Humanity, 67
hypoventilation, 10, 34

I

Immortality, 47, 71–72
Incarnation, 70, 71, 72–73
Index, Bible, 40, 41
Index, Proscribed, 35
inventions, 17–18, 28
iron, 24, 31
Italy, 34–35

J

Jesus Christ (see also Lord), 39, 71, 73
Julian calendar, 8

K

Kant, Immanuel, 48, **53**, 53–54
　Critique of Pure Reason, 54
　Dreams of a Spirit-Seer, 53
　Letter to Charlotte von Knobloch, 48
Karlscrona, 20
Kemper, Johan, 4

L

Lamburg, Bishop Eric, 55
Last Judgment, 74
Latin, 16, 18, 39
Leeuwenhoek, Anton van, 16–17, 33
Leiden, 16, 17, 27

Leipzig, 28, 32, 36
lens grinding, 17
Liege, 27
Linköping, 33
Linnaeus, Carolus, 4, 35, 36, 62
London, 13–15, 17, 36, 39–41, 43, 61–62
longitude, 15, 16
Lord, 8, 39–40, 44, 45, 47, 51, 59, 64, 65, 68, 69, 71, 74
Louisa Ulrika (Queen of Sweden), 48, 58
love, 66–67, 72
Lund, 20
Lutheran(s), 5, 9, 40, 51, 55, 57–58, 63

M

Malpighi, Marcello, 33
marriage, 28, 55, 68
mathematics, 17, 20, 28, 40
Maximus Homo, 72
Messiah, 4
Messiter, Dr. Husband, 61
metallurgy, 29
metals, 27, 28
microscope, **17**
Milan, 35
mining, 4, **6**, 18, 24, 27, 31
Mines, Board of (see Board of Mines)
monarchy, 3, 26
monotheism, 67
moon, 15
Moraeus, Johan, 6, 36
motor functions, 38
Museum of Mining, 28
Museum of Technology, 28

N

nebular hypothesis, 31
nervous system, 36
new church, 47, 74
Newton, Sir Isaac, vii, 15
Nicea, Council of, 65
Norway, 20
Norwegian, 13

O

observatory, 15–16
Oetinger, Friedrich Christoph,
    *Swedenborg and Others
    Compared*, 50
other-world experiences, 40
Oxford, 16

P

Padua, University of, 35
Paris, 6, 17, 34
Paris National Observatory, **33**
Particle, Swedenborg's drawing of, **iv**
Peace Congress, 17
philosophers, 32, 53
physics, 28, 33
physiological studies, 34, 36
Pietism, 9
poetry, 16
Polhem, Christopher, viii, 19–21, 28
Polhem, Emerentia, 20
portrait, of Swedenborg, **11**, 32
Prague, 31
Proscribed Index, 35

Q

quarantine, 13

R

rationality, 67, 69
reality, 66, 67, 72
religion(s), vii, 4, 45, 64, 71
reproductive system, 36
resurrection, 74
revelation, 64, 69
Riddarholmen (Street), 34
Riksdag, 24, 28, 31, 35
Riddarhaus, **23**, 24, 28, 29
Robinson, Bishop John, 17
rolling mills, 24, 27
Rome, 35
Rosen, Dr. Johan, 55, 58
Rostock, 17, 18
Royal Gardens at Stockholm, **46**
Royal Greenwich Observatory, **15**
Rudbeck, Olof, 4, 18
Ruysch, Fred., 33

S

saltworks, 21
Sandels, Samuel, 62
Saurian fossil, 31–32
science, viii, 6, 14, 16, 20, 39, 43, 64, 66
scientific, viii, 4, 5, 19, 28, 44, 64
Scripture, 41–44, 49, 57, 63, 69, 73
Second Coming, 74
self-criticism, 37
sensation, 33
shamanism, Lappish, 4
Shearsmith, Richard, 61

ship, 13–14, 48, 62
Skara, 5, 7, 32
Skinnskatteberg, 25
smelters, 25, 28
smelting, 25, 27, 31
soul, vii, 33, 35, 36
spirit(s), 9, 61, 66, 71, 72
spiritual, 10, 41–44, 54, 55, 57, 59,
   62–64, 68–72, 74
Starbo, 19, 25
Steuch, Kristina Maria, 28
Stierncrona, Elizabet, 29
Stockholm, 7–8, **8–9**, 21, 28, 31,
   42, 43, 48
Stora Kopparberg (see also Great
   Copper Mountain, 20–21
Stora Nygatan, 29
summerhouse, **41**
Sveden, 7, 35
Svindersvik, 50, **52**
Swedberg, Albert, 7
Swedberg, Katherina, 7
Swedberg, Daniel, 7
Swedberg, Eliezer, 7
Swedberg, Jesper, viii, 5, 7–11, 25, 32
Swedberg, Jesper, Jr., 7
Swedberg, Margaretha, 8
Swedberg, Peter, 7
Swedberg, Sara (Behm), 7, 21, 25
Swedberg, Sara (Bergia), 10, 21, 25
Sweden, 3, 6, 8, 13, 15, 17–21, 24, 27, 29,
   32, 36, 48, 61, 62
Swedenborg coat of arms, **22**
Swedenborg, works of
   Animal Kingdom, 36
   Apocalypse Explained, 48, 49, 50, 51
   Apocalypse Revealed, 52
   Arcana Coelestia, 43, 45, 47, 49, 50, 52,
     53, 54, 57
   Balance of Trade, 28
   Brief Exposition, 57
   Continuation on the Last Judgment, **51**
   Coronis, 61
   Divine Love and Wisdom, 51, 58
   Divine Providence, 51, 52
   Doctrine of Faith, 54
   Doctrine of Life, 54
   Doctrine of Sacred Scripture, 53
   Doctrine of the Lord, 51, 65
   Dynamics of the Soul's Domain, 35
   Earths in the Universe, 45, 47
   Economy of the Animal Kingdom, 35, 36
   Festivus Applausus, 18
   First Principles of Natural Things, 31
   Four Doctrines, 51, 57
   Heaven and Hell, 45, 47, 54

   Heavenly Mysteries, 43
   *Inflation and Deflation of Swedish
     Money, The,* 28
   Journal of Dreams, 37
   Last Judgment, 47
   Marriage Love, 52, 55
   *New Jerusalem and its Heavenly
     Doctrine,* 45, 47
   *New Method of Finding the
     Longitudes, A,* 20
   Noble and Base Metals, 28
   On Copper and Brass, 31
   On Iron and Steel, 31
   On the Height of Waters, 33
   On Tremulation, 33
   *Philosophical and Mineralogical
     Works,* 31, 32, 35
   Posthumous Theological Works, 61
   Preface to Principles of Chemistry, 27
   Scripture Confirmations, 57
   *Selected Sentences from L. Annaeus
     Seneca and Publius Syrus the Mime,
     with Notes,* 11
   Soul-Body Interaction, 57
   Spiritual Diary, **38,** 40, 42
   Soul's Domain, 36
   True Christian Religion, 57, 59, 61, 64,
     65
   White Horse of the Apocolypse, 45,
     45, 47, 50
   Word Explained, 38
   Worship and Love of God, 39
Swedish Academy of Sciences, 35, 62

T

Tessin, Count Carl Gustav, 35, 50
theological, 9, 10, 26, 31, 36, 40, 44, 45,
   47, 50, 54, 55, 61, 63, 64, 70
theology, 3, 7, 9, 32, 49, 52, 55, 57, 58,
   65, 68, 71, 73, 74
theophany, **38,** 39
thought-world, 47
Torino, 35
Trollhattan Canal, 21
Tuxen, General Christian, 61

U

Ulrika Eleonora (Queen of Sweden),
   8, 23
universal human, 72
Universality, 71
Uppsala, University at, vii, **viii,** 3–5,
   9–11, 19, 28, 43, 62
Utrecht, 17

V

Varnhem, 32
Vatican Library, 35
Venice, 35
Versailles, 17
Vieussens, Raymond, 33
vision(s), 39–40, 61
von Knoblock, Charlotte, 48

W

watchmaking, 14
wisdom, 66–70, 72, 74
Word made flesh, 73
world, physical, 5, 47, 66–67, 71
world, spiritual, 40, 59, 64, 70, 72, 74